EFT FOR
(POSTTRAUMATIC STRESS DISORDER)

by Dawson Church, PhD

www.EFTUniverse.com

Energy Psychology Press
3340 Fulton Rd., #442, Fulton, CA 95439
www.EFTUniverse.com

Cataloging-in-Publication Data
Church, Dawson, 1956–
EFT for PTSD / Dawson Church. — 4th ed.
    p. cm.
Includes bibliographical references and index.
ISBN (print) 978-1-60415-216-6; (e-book) 978-1-60415-266-1
1. Posttraumatic stress disorder—Treatment. I. Title.
RC552.P67C73 2008
616.85'2106—dc22
              2008046923

This book demonstrates an impressive personal improvement tool. It is not a substitute for training in psychology or psychotherapy. The author urges the reader to use these techniques under the supervision of a qualified therapist or physician. The author and publisher do not assume responsibility for how the reader chooses to apply the techniques herein. The ideas, procedures, and suggestions in this book are not intended as a substitute for consultation with your professional health care provider. If you have any questions about whether or not to use EFT, consult your physician or licensed mental health practitioner. The information in this book is of a general nature only, and may not be used to treat or diagnose any particular disease or any particular person. Reading this book does not constitute a professional relationship or professional advice or services. No endorsement or warranty is explicit or implied by any entity connected to this book, and there is no guarantee that you will have the same results.

Cover design by Victoria Valentine
Editing by Stephanie Marohn
Typesetting by Karin Kinsey
Typeset in Cochin and Adobe Garamond
Printed in USA by Bang Printing
Fourth Edition

10 9 8 7 6 5 4 3 2 1

Contents

Chapter 1: A Quick Start Guide to
Using EFT for PTSD 11

Giving You Hope 12

My Story.. 13

EFT Resolves 35 Years of PTSD
by Winston "Brad" Scott 18

EFT Helps Heal Rape Trauma
by Angela Amias 22

Tapping 25

Your First Experience with EFT: Try It Now 27

EFT as an Evidence-Based Practice 30

Clinical EFT 32

The Evidence for EFT Treatment of PTSD.......... 33

Applying EFT.. 35

Chapter 2: About Posttraumatic Stress Disorder........ 37

Pervasive Psychological Trauma 37

Attachment: Secure vs. Disorganized 39

Trauma Is Physical as Well as Psychological 43

Stress Is Hormonal as Well as Neurological 46

Your Body Can't Tell the Difference 49

Driven to Distraction by Your Cortex................... 51

Bringing the Traumatized Brain Back Online....... 53

Stroking Your Inner Dog 57

PTSD, Anxiety, and Depression as
    Chemical Imbalances in the Brain................... 58

The VA Could Have Remediated PTSD for
    Half the Cost of One Drug 61

The Future of Psychology and Medicine.............. 78

Chapter 3: How to Do EFT: The Basic Recipe........... 81

Testing.. 86

The Setup Statement... 89

Psychological Reversal.. 90

Affirmation... 92

Secondary Gain 96

How EFT Corrects for Psychological Reversal 97

The Sequence 98

The Reminder Phrase 99

If Your SUD Level Doesn't Come Down to 0.... 101

EFT for You and Others 102

The Importance of Targeting Specific Events..... 103

Tapping on Aspects 105

Finding Core Issues 107

The Generalization Effect...................................... 108

The Movie Technique and
    Tell the Story Technique 111

Constricted Breathing 116

The Personal Peace Procedure 117

Is It Working Yet? 120

Saying the Right Words 122

The Next Steps on Your EFT Journey 123

Chapter 4: Options and Variations 127

Additional Points for the Full Basic Recipe 128

The 9 Gamut Point and Procedure 131

Excessive Emotionality in a Brain-Damaged
   Child *by Tana Clark* 134

The Sore Spot 135

A Few Optional Points 136

Putting It All Together 137

More About the Acceptance Phrase 142

Soft Language to Ease the EFT Acceptance
   Phrase *by Betty Moore-Hafter* 145

More Notes on Positive Setups 149

The Apex Effect 150

Borrowing Benefits 151

Chapter 5: Tapping for PTSD 155

Example of the Basic Recipe Applied to a
   General Description 156

Example of the Basic Recipe Applied to a
   Specific Memory 158

Rapid Relief from Accident Flashbacks
   by Ann Adams 160

Resolution of Vertigo and a Car Crash Memory
   by Edward Miner 164

Chapter 6: The Gentle Techniques 167
    The Need for Gentle Techniques 170
    The Four Characteristics of a Traumatic Event .. 172
    The Trauma Capsule 177
    Cognitive Processing: Shifts and How to
        Identify Them 178
    Dissociation 183
    Inducing Dissociation 185
    Tearless Trauma Technique 186
    Using the Tearless Trauma Technique in a
        Group *by Steve Wells* 189
    Further Layers of Therapeutic Dissociation 190
    Exceptions to the Rule of Being Specific 192
    Sneaking Up on the Problem 193
    Chasing the Pain 197
    Sneaking Away from the Problem 199
    Touch and Breathe (TAB) 201
    Posttraumatic Growth 202
Chapter 7: Improving EFT's Effectiveness 205
    The Tap-While-You-Gripe Technique
        by Rick Wilkes 207
    Can You Do EFT Incorrectly? 210
    Conditions That Interfere 212
    Self-Talk and the Writings on Your Walls 212
    Tail-Enders 213
    Saying Goodbye to the Past 215
    How to Tell Whether EFT Is Working 215

Chapter 8: Terrorist Attacks and Other
    Nightmares.. 221
  EFT and the Aftermath of 9/11
    by Dr. Carol Look... 222
  EFT for a Hurricane Katrina Survivor
    by Rebecca Marina 229
  EFT Resolves Earthquake PTSD in 2 Sessions
    by Karen Degen... 231
  Where Only the Pros Should Tread
    by Lori Lorenz 234

Chapter 9: EFT for Combat PTSD............................ 239
  A Vet Tells His Story
    by Evan Hessel.. 239
  From a Downward to an Upward Spiral
    by Olli 242
  How EFT Helps Active-Duty Warriors
    by Dr. Constance Louie-Handelman 245
  Tapping for Collections of Traumas
    by Lindsay Kenny 248
  Introducing EFT to Combat Veterans
    by Ingrid Dinter 256

Chapter 10: Do-It-Yourself EFT 263
  Accident Victim Resolves Her Own
    PTSD 40 Years Later *by Pat Farrell*.............. 268
  How I Handled My Child Abuse PTSD
    All by Myself *by Lisa Rogers*............................ 271
  Paramedic Cures His Own PTSD
    by Bob Patefield.. 275

References 279

Index... 291

A Quick Start Guide to Using EFT for PTSD

If you're reading this book, it's for one of three reasons.

1. You have been diagnosed with posttraumatic stress disorder (PTSD) or you suspect you might have PTSD.

2. A family member of yours has PTSD. Perhaps your husband, wife, daughter, or son is a veteran with PSTD. Perhaps a family member has PTSD as the result of a car crash, assault, or some other traumatic event. Perhaps you suspect the erratic behavior of your spouse is due to childhood abuse. You're motivated to find out more and to help a loved one.

3. You work with people who have PTSD.

No one picks up a book called *EFT for PTSD* for light recreational reading. I know you need answers, and I'm here to give them to you. This book gets right to the point.

It summarizes the work of the world's top experts in PTSD and EFT. I'm going to tell you, bluntly and frankly, what's possible and what's not. I'm going to lay out why PTSD is such an insidious disease, why it gets worse over time without proper treatment, how it devastates families, marriages, and communities, and what sort of changes you can realistically expect if you learn and practice EFT.

Giving You Hope

This book was also written to give you hope. A huge amount of time went in to writing it, into inviting top people in their fields to share their expertise, and into soliciting stories from members of the EFT community about their direct experiences with PTSD. All these people contributed because they want to give hope to those who suffer from PTSD.

You need hope when you're dealing with PTSD. As we'll discover together in the coming chapters, PTSD is a devastating condition. It's not just bad for the person diagnosed. It affects brothers, sisters, husbands, wives, sons, and daughters. Its effects spread out to the whole community (McFarlane & van der Kolk, 2007).

PTSD often becomes worse over time. The reason for this is that it changes the brain. The parts of the brain responsible for learning and happiness actually shrink, while cognitive function and memory degrade (Peters et al., 2010; Hedges & Woon, 2010; Felmingham et al., 2009). A veteran may show no symptoms for a year or two after returning from combat but then develop PTSD. Family members of Vietnam veterans often notice them getting worse 30 or 40 years later. All those years of building up the neural circuitry of stress increases its efficiency, while those parts of the brain responsible for learning and memory wither away. It's not a pretty picture in the long term, and it's a problem that does not go away if you ignore it.

With Emotional Freedom Techniques (EFT), there is real and tangible hope. I helped start a nonprofit a few years back called the Veterans Stress Project, and we've now worked with more than 10,000 veterans and family members with PTSD. Many of them report full recoveries, and you can read their stories at StressProject.org.

We've also performed a series of scientific studies, and the results from these are consistent: close to 90% of veterans who use EFT recover from PTSD. Not only do their symptoms improve after treatment, but also the results hold over time. Once they're healed, they don't go back.

These studies, published in peer-reviewed professional journals and performed to rigorous experimental standards, demonstrate that the stories you'll read in this book aren't the exception, they're the rule. These aren't a few isolated successes in a sea of failures; that 90% success rate is typical. Yes, there are some sufferers who try EFT and don't get better, but they are a small minority.

My Story

First, I need to make a confession. I have struggled with PTSD most of my adult life. I have never told this story publicly; I'm telling it now for the first time.

I didn't know I had PTSD till I was in my late 40s. I always knew I'd blanked out my childhood from 0 to around 10 because it was too horrible to remember. I have three memories from the age of 5, one from the age of 7, and one from the age of 10. I have a few from the ages of 12 to 15, and none of them are good.

One 5-year-old memory is fairly detailed. I'm walking to kindergarten through the snow, carrying my lunchbox. I'm looking down at my shoes, and dragging them through the snow to create a trail, rather than picking them up to plant nice crisp footprints in the white powder. I'm dragging my feet because I'm terrified of what I'm about to encounter.

My father was working at the Castle, a missionary establishment in Colorado Springs. We'd just moved to the United States, and I was enrolled in Howbert Elementary School. I didn't fit in. I had the wrong accent and the wrong clothes. Our family had no money, so my clothes came from the "missionary barrel" at church. That's a place where other families discard their unwanted clothes.

But my mother did not allow me to select anything I wanted from the missionary barrel. I was only permitted to select one garment every few weeks, and I'd learned that selecting the best was frowned upon as "vanity," one of the Seven Deadly Sins. Once I had my heart set on a warm jacket, but when my mother saw it, she forced me to put it back. By the age of 5, I'd been trained to select the worst of the cast-off clothes. So I went to school dressed in the scrapings from the bottom of the missionary barrel. Even my lunchbox was a discarded oddity meant for a younger child. I sat alone in the playground during breaks. I didn't know the culture, and didn't know how to make friends.

Among the other indignities Howbert heaped on me was a diagnosis that I needed remedial speech education, presumably to correct my British accent. The speech education classes certainly produced an effect. Shamed for the way I expressed myself, I developed a stutter, a fear of public speaking, a sense of worthlessness, an aversion to being seen or heard, and a lifelong speech impediment.

My mother was not a happy person. During a physical exam many years ago, the doctor asked me how I came to have scars from second- and third- degree burns on my face and body. Like most of the rest of my childhood, I could remember nothing. While there are blank spaces where my early memories should be, I do have a recollection of the emotional tone of living with my mother: sheer terror.

I realized I had PTSD when in my 40s I began to work with veterans. As I read their lists of symptoms, I saw myself in them. At that time I was also in an abusive relationship, and when it ended, I felt like I had awakened from a dream. I realized I'd been selecting relationship partners who were either emotionally dead, which felt safe, or emotionally expressive though abusive. I'd chosen either people who were the exact opposite of my mother, or exactly like my mother. I'd carried the trauma of my past into my present.

Virginia Satir was a legendary therapist of the 20th century and one of the founders of the field of marriage and family therapy. She defined a marriage as two sets of dysfunctional family patterns coming together to perpetuate themselves into the next generation.

I was a poster child for her bleak prognosis. Till my late 40s, I trembled at the thought of making a public speech. I was married for a long time to a partner whose default setting was criticism, and seemed incapable of kind or supportive words. This gradually eroded what little self-esteem I had. After a decade in that marriage, I believed I was worthless, with no value in the world, and with nothing important to say. As a child, I acquired the core belief that that my entire life was a mistake, and I should never have been born. I chose a wife who reinforced my self-estimation.

I also had many other characteristics of PTSD. I was completely out of touch with my body. I regarded it as little more than an unattractive platform for carrying my head around. I'd gone to school dances as a teenager, and besides feeling shut down with embarrassment, I could not move my limbs with any sort of grace or coordination. I also could not distinguish right from left, and I often transposed digits in numbers and letters in words.

When I began to spend time with people other than my ex-wife, I slowly began to realize that not everyone responded to me with criticism; in fact, many people valued what I brought to the conversation.

Within a few years, I had tapped away most of my fears with EFT. I had established a regular meditation practice. I had written a best-selling book, *The Genie in Your Genes.* I was speaking at many medical and psychological conferences each year, and through radio and online shows I was speaking to up to 10 million people annually. Often I received standing ovations. I received many letters and e-mails from people telling me that my work had completely changed their lives. I changed my whole career path from focusing on early retirement to focusing on brining this work to as many people as possible. In addition to the Veterans Stress Project, I founded the National Institute for Integrative Healthcare, started Energy Psychology Press, and assembled the largest archive of EFT stories online at EFT Universe.

Today I'm remarried to a woman who loves me unconditionally. She sits in the front row when I deliver keynote speeches, her eyes shining with love. After every speech, she holds me close while telling me how wonderfully I spoke and how blessed people in the audience felt. If I feel I performed under par, she tells me that nobody noticed. Even after many years together, when we travel to new places, strangers often mistake us for newlyweds. We give thanks every day when we wake up to the miracle of love in which we live.

Since starting this journey of healing, my life has changed completely in every dimension. If I can heal, you can too!

In this book, I hope to inspire you with the stories of many people who, like me, have reclaimed their lives from the ravages of PTSD and set themselves up for a whole new future. There are many stories in the book, as well as a summary of the research evidence showing that EFT can rehabilitate people with PTSD.

Here are two stories of other people who've used EFT to address their PTSD symptoms. In the first account, Winston Scott, a certified clinical hypnotherapist, writes about how he used EFT to help a firefighter who suffered from posttraumatic stress—not as a result of the stress in his profession but from a childhood trauma that occurred when he was 3 years old.

EFT Resolves 35 Years of PTSD

By Winston "Brad" Scott, CCHT

At an EFT seminar in Boston, I had a lunchtime encounter with a local firefighter. My friend and I went out to get some non-hotel food and saw a deli across the road. There was a fire truck parked beside it, so we thought it had to have good eats. After we entered and saw the long line, we knew this was probably true.

I ended up standing beside a fireman and, just making small talk, told him he was the reason we were here. He wondered about this and we told him. "If the fire department eats here, then it must be good food." He noted that we weren't "from around here" (he had a very strong Bostonian accent and I live in Canada) and asked what brought us down this way. Instead of trying to explain EFT at that point, I just said I was a hypnotherapist (most people understand that easily) and I was at a seminar to learn about a great new stress management tool.

He looked at me questioningly and then blurted out that I should be using him as my "monkey." I asked him what he meant and he said that he felt completely stressed out and was seriously feeling—and these are his words—"ready to jump."

Of course, I asked him what was up. He proceeded to tell me that he had buried seven brothers (firemen) in the last 7 weeks and he was just too young for this and constantly in a highly stressed state. He didn't think he could "take any more."

I noticed then that the muscles in his neck and jaw were all clenched. I thought, if he is that stressed waiting for a sandwich, then EFT is going to be his new best friend. I asked him if he would like to experiment and check out the technique. He said that he would be at the firehall for the next 8 hours barring a fire and would be more than willing to try anything, as he was desperate. He told me that if I was willing, we could check it out, but he doubted it would help.

I have a total respect for firefighters, as my grandfather was a captain in the Toronto fire department, so I decided to skip a little of the seminar and go over.

We met at the door of the station and he took me back to a private area with a couple of seats.

This next part is a testament to getting yourself out of the way. I went in there thinking that it was a current issue that was stressing him (the loss of his "brothers" in such a short period). This proves that to attack any problem with a preconceived notion is a mistake. We started tapping around that issue, using the basic shortcut method, but didn't get a lot of movement.

Because we weren't really getting anywhere, I decided to ask a favorite EFT question: If there was one thing in your life you could eliminate or do over, what would it be? There was no hesitation. He had his issue immediately. It turned out that, at the age of 3, he believed that he had killed his best friend. Two of his friends and he had snuck in to a swimming pool. To use his words, "Three went in and only two came out." His belief was he killed his friend. He believed he must have pushed his friend in because that is the kind of thing he would have done. He didn't actually remember it. He just believed he did and he believed that he should be punished and held accountable for it. He didn't feel he had the right to a happy life.

This brave man had been living with posttraumatic stress for 35 of his 38 years. He told me he had never really "felt right inside," so we tapped on several aspects of this incident. Whenever he got "stuck," I used the 9 Gamut Procedure and immediately his SUD level dropped significantly. I know a lot of people have shelved the 9 Gamut, but when you get stuck, it is a remarkable tool.

I don't want to go into what we tapped on as it is a very personal story and the details might not respect his right to privacy. Suffice to say that, 40 minutes later, he thanked me, gave me a hug, and told me that he had been to every doctor in town and hadn't been able to resolve anything. He said he felt as if a great weight had been taken off his shoulders. He looked like a different person.

His jawline was relaxed. His neck muscles weren't knotted and sticking out.

I felt really honored to be able to show such a brave man the power of EFT and that there was a way to truly let go of all the destructive trauma and guilt.

I feel very privileged to call this man my friend. We have stayed in touch and, months later, he reports that he still feels very calm about the situation. He commented, "Hey, I've done my time. I really do deserve some peace."

I am so in awe of EFT and the peace it can bring about.

❊ ❊ ❊

Notice that the fireman's immediate distress was linked to burying seven fellow firefighters in the previous 7 weeks, but that the practitioner wasn't getting anywhere using EFT on those deaths. They didn't make progress until the practitioner asked a key question of the kind you'll be trained to ask in this book. That led to the identification of an underlying event that was the true cause of the fireman's stress.

Also notice that his distress about the current deaths was resolved when he tapped on the childhood event. They never even needed to tap on the current events. The reason adult events disturb us is almost always because they recapitulate losses we suffered as children. Until we dig deep, and uncover those early causes, trying to feel better about the current situation is usually not successful. But when we resolve the early trauma, the later ones automatically diminish in emotional impact.

In the next account, certified EFT practitioner Angela Amias writes about a session during which the client made the connection between a current vision problem and a past unhealed rape trauma, and cleared both with EFT.

EFT Helps Heal Rape Trauma

By Angela Amias, LISW, EFT INT-1

At times, past trauma can manifest itself in the physical body in unexpected ways.

In this case, Josie, a client in her 30s, was working through persistent negative feelings about the break-up of a relationship that had occurred a few years prior to our work together. In addition, and seemingly unrelated to this issue, she had recently been experiencing unusual problems with her vision, for which physicians had been unable to find any physical explanation.

While discussing her feelings about the break-up during one session, Josie said that what really bothered her about the relationship was "I never felt like I had any control." After tapping briefly on the phrase, "Even though I had no control, I deeply love and accept myself," she stopped and reported that she was having trouble with her vision again.

Everything in her visual field seemed to be tilting to the left.

She said, "It's like I'm not seeing things correctly."

This was making it difficult for her to focus on our work.

At this point, neither of us made a connection between the issues we were discussing and this visual problem, but since the client was distressed by the visual disturbance, we decided to try EFT to see if it might have an effect.

We tapped on:

Even though I'm not seeing things correctly, I deeply love and accept myself.

As Josie continued tapping on the phrase *"I'm not seeing things correctly,"* she suddenly began to cry and told me she was experiencing visual flashbacks of a sexual assault that had occurred in her early 20s.

While she had mentioned this experience before, she had downplayed the event, describing it as an unpleasant sexual experience rather than rape, because it had occurred within the context of a long-term relationship. Now, however, her intensity was very high and we tapped for several minutes without speaking until she was calmer and said she was ready to work through this memory.

When I asked her to guess at the intensity of the experience without thinking directly about it, she rated it a 10. We tapped until it was at a 5 and then I asked her to pretend this experience was a movie and give it a title. I reminded her not to watch the movie in her mind but just focus on the title.

She gave it the title "Man rapes woman" and rated her intensity about the title at an 8. After tapping on this title for a few rounds, her intensity increased to a 10 and she said, "I really hate the word 'rape.'" So we switched from tapping on the title to tapping on the word "rape,"

"Even though I really hate that word…" to *"Even though I hate the word 'rape'…"* until her intensity around that word had dropped to a 1.

We then tapped on the title until it had also dropped to a 1.

At this point, we were ready to begin working through the actual traumatic event. In order to prevent Josie from being flooded by emotions or possibly reexperiencing the event, we created several barriers between her and the experience. She imagined the movie on a movie screen, pulled curtains across the screen, and imagined she was in a separate building far from the theatre where this movie was playing.

Only at this point, when safety had been established, did we slowly work through the experience, tapping on each part of the story that contained an emotional charge before moving to the next part. By the end of the session, she was able to tell the entire story of her experience without experiencing any emotional intensity.

Rape is a violation of the fundamental integrity of one's own body.

Looking back, it's easy to see the connection between this experience and Josie's difficulty getting over a relationship in which she felt this lack of control in other ways. Because she had actively suppressed her feelings about this experience for several years, it had been difficult for her to understand why she was having such a hard time with her recent break-up.

Her description of her visual problem, "I'm not seeing things clearly," was a perfect metaphor for her inability to see the connection between her current emotional experience and this past unhealed trauma.

Once that trauma was uncovered and healed, she no longer needed the physical symptom to get her attention. In fact, after working though all the aspects of this trauma, Josie experienced no further episodes of visual disturbance.

✿ ✿ ✿

These aren't isolated stories. As you read this book, you'll see the accounts of many more people who healed in this way. Your hope will grow, and it will be well founded. If you're trying EFT for the first time, you'll be amazed by how quickly you can heal traumatic memories. With practice, you'll look back on your life, as I did, and find you've become a different person.

Tapping

EFT is often called "tapping" because one of its key components is tapping with your fingertips on acupuncture points on your body. Acupuncture has been proven effective for a variety of problems in many scientific studies (Braverman, 2004). Those problems include physical symptoms such as pain as well as psychological problems such as PTSD.

While acupressure points (shortened to "acupoints") can be stimulated by inserting needles at those points, they can also be stimulated without needles. One example is the Japanese massage method called Shiatsu, which massages the points by hand. In this chapter, I'll show you how to stimulate a series of acupoints on your own body by tapping on them with your fingertips. Pressure on acupoints seems to have much the same effect as needling them (Cherkin et al., 2009).

Acupuncture theory teaches that energy flows through our body along pathways called meridians. These have been mapped using modern scientific instrumentation (Schlebusch, Maric-Oehler, & Popp, 2005). Disease can be caused by a blockage or interruption of that flow, and acupuncture or acupressure can be used to remove those blockages. In the early 1960s, an American chiropractor named George Goodheart discovered that he could successfully treat physical problems by tapping on acupoints (Adams & Davidson, 2011), and a clinical psychologist named Roger Callahan developed a system of acupoint tapping for psychological problems (Callahan, 2000).

One of Callahan's students, Gary Craig, abbreviated Callahan's system and named it EFT (Craig & Fowlie, 1995). That's the same method we'll practice throughout this book. It's fully described in the current edition of *The EFT Manual* (Church, 2013), though we'll give you enough information in this book for you to use it yourself effectively.

This book also includes a chapter on "The Gentle Techniques" reprinted from *The EFT Manual*. These are three specialized EFT techniques designed for working with trauma. They allow you to process even highly traumatic events quickly and easily. Though the Gentle Techniques are easy to learn and apply, research and clinical practice have shown that they are phenomenally effective at permanently resolving the symptoms of PTSD.

Your First Experience with EFT: Try It Now

Are you ready to try EFT yourself? I like to show people how to do EFT first, rather than engage in long-winded explanations. When you have your first tangible experience of how fast it can heal a psychological wound, you'll be a believer. There's an old Hermetic saying that goes like this: "For the person who's not had the experience, no explanation is possible. For the person who's had the experience, no explanation is necessary." EFT is like that. Doing it even one time gives you a "felt sense" in your body of the kind of relief it can offer you, even if you're working on a burden you've carried for a long time and believe it's impossible to lift. You'll be surprised at how far and how fast you can heal with EFT.

Here's a very simple way to do EFT for the first time that will give you a sense of its potential. It's going to take you less than 2 minutes. I'm going to keep it as simple as possible, and I'm also going to give you a practical tool to measure whether or not EFT is working for you. I'd like you to think about a traumatic memory. Pick one that's safe to work on, one that you know from past experience won't send you into a tailspin. Pick an event that took five minutes or less to occur, and one that you can label with a title. If it were a movie, what would the movie title be?

Rate the severity of your emotional distress on a scale from 0 to 10. Zero indicates no distress whatsoever; you can think about the memory and feel completely calm. Ten indicates emotional agony. In EFT we call this score your SUD or Subjective Units of Distress (Wolpe, 1958). Write down your SUD score here:

Movie Title _____

SUD Before EFT _____

Use the accompanying illustration to locate the first tapping point on the side of your hand. We call this the Karate Chop point. Lightly but firmly, tap there with the fingertips of the other hand while repeating this phrase: "Even though I experienced [movie title], I deeply and completely accept myself." You don't have to believe this statement, since EFT is not dependent on your level of belief. Simply say the words.

Karate Chop (KC) point.

Keep tapping, and repeat that phrase three times.

Then, tap on the following points with two fingers of either hand 7 to 10 times, on either side of the body, while repeating the title of your movie.

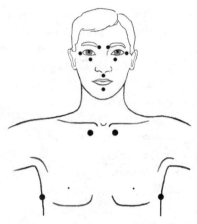

EB, SE, UE, UN, Ch, CB and UA points.

After tapping on all these points, tune back in to movie. Rerun it in your mind. Write down your new SUD level here:

SUD After First EFT Sequence _____

The chances are good that your SUD level is much lower than it was before. It may not be at a 0 yet, however, so let's apply EFT once more. While tapping your Karate Chop point, say, "Even though I still have some distress about [movie title], I deeply and completely accept myself." Repeat this two more times while tapping that same point. Then, repeat your movie title while tapping on every point with 2 fingertips. Really tune in to the details of your movie while you do this.

When you're finished, write down your new SUD level:

SUD After Second EFT Sequence _____

The likelihood is that your SUD is now much lower than before. Perhaps it's even down to 0. If it's not entirely gone, no problem, since you've just tried the most elementary form of EFT. As you read Chapter 3 and improve your skills with EFT, you'll get better and better at applying it. If you're like most people who do this simple and quick exercise, you're probably quite surprised by how fast your emotional pain diminished. This can encourage you to read further, and start to unlock the many deep healing benefits of EFT.

In the next part of this chapter, we'll look at some of the highlights of research into EFT for PTSD. We'll also discuss the standards for "evidence-based" practices published by the American Psychological Association (APA) and how these apply to EFT research and treatment. These are important and interesting topics, but if you'd like to plunge straight into doing more EFT, then jump to Chapter 3, "How to Do EFT: The Basic Recipe." It will walk you, step by step, through doing EFT yourself.

EFT as an Evidence-Based Practice

What does the phrase "evidence-based" mean, and why is it important? Much of modern medicine is based on solid science, but a surprising amount of it is not. Many medical procedures are performed more out of habit or belief than anything else. One example comes from the practice of knee surgery.

One surgeon wanted to compare the two most popular forms of knee surgery to determine which was best, so he performed a randomized controlled trial (RCT) pitting one against the other (Moseley, 2002). To control for the placebo effect, in which a patient's belief has a healing influence all by itself, he introduced a third group. This group received sham surgery. They were sedated, wheeled into the operating room, incisions were made in their knees just as if they were receiving a real treatment, and they were then sewn up again.

To his great surprise, the placebo group that received the sham surgery did just as well as the other two groups on most measures. At that time knee surgery was an $11-billion-per-year industry in the United States, but that huge expense was being incurred without any clear scientific support.

In fact, the editor of the prestigious peer-reviewed journal the *New England Journal of Medicine* editorialized that medical journals, rather than purveying sound science, had become "primarily a marketing machine" for Big Pharma which was co-opting "every institution that might stand in its way" (Angell, 2005, p. 336). Richard Horton, editor of the Lancet, wrote: "Journals have devolved into information laundering operations for the pharmaceutical industry" (Horton, 2004). When you compare the possible benefits of the treatments they promote against the harm they do and the side effects, Franz Ingelfinger, another editor of the *New England Journal of Medicine* said that the balance is about zero (Ingelfinger, 1977). This is why it's important to determine that any proposed treatment has scientific merit before implementing it.

Clinical EFT

EFT for PTSD and the other books in this series are companions to *The EFT Manual* (Church, 2013). You'll find EFT's fundamental method, called the Basic Recipe, described in detail in Chapter 3 of this book. That's the same form of EFT described in *The EFT Manual,* and the one you just tried from the instructions in this chapter. That form of EFT was used in all the studies cited here, and since it's been validated by much research, we call it Clinical EFT. There are many variants of EFT in the marketplace, but the only one that is backed by many years of scientific study is Clinical EFT. That's why if you do EFT as described in this book and *The EFT Manual,* you can have the confidence of knowing you're using the exact same method that's been proven to work in that whole large body of research.

Clinical EFT will train you to ask the kinds of probing questions that Brad Scott asked the firefighter when they were getting nowhere tapping on the recent deaths. Whenever I hear someone say, "I used EFT and it didn't work," deeper inquiry reveals that they'd used a superficial variant of EFT, and not Clinical EFT. When I then use the full arsenal of tools we offer in Clinical EFT on the problem, even though EFT "didn't work" in the past, the client usually has a massive breakthrough.

The books in this EFT series also abide by the standards of the American Psychological Association (APA) in terms of style, ethics, and proof. The Clinical Psychology division of the APA (Division 12) published standards for "empirically validated treatments"

(Chambless & Hollon, 1998)—"APA standards," for short—and EFT meets those standards for a wide variety of psychological problems including anxiety, depression, PTSD, and phobias (Feinstein, 2012).

The Evidence for EFT Treatment of PTSD

Several studies of EFT have shown it to be very effective for PTSD. A hospital in Britain's NHS (National Health Service) compared EFT to Eye Movement Desensitization and Reprocessing (EMDR), another excellent method (Karatzias et al., 2011). Both EMDR and EFT were also compared to treatment as usual (TAU). The investigators found that patients receiving either EFT or EMDR recovered in an average of four sessions, while those receiving TAU did not get better at all. This was a startling result since most conventional treatments for PTSD take much longer than four sessions and are not nearly as successful.

This result was echoed in another RCT comparing TAU with TAU plus EFT. It found that 86% of veterans recovered from PTSD after six sessions, with 80% still recovered when followed up in 3 and 6 months (Church, Hawk, et al., 2013). The drop in PTSD symptoms was a dramatic 64%. This study was replicated by an independent research team (Geronilla, McWilliams, & Clond, 2014), with essentially the same results. The APA standards require two RCTs in order for a treatment to qualify as "empirically validated" and, at this point, EFT has more than met that burden of proof.

Data from the Church, Hawk, et al. (2013) study were also examined in greater detail by other researchers in order to glean other useful information about how to best bring EFT to veterans. It was found that 67% of veterans recover after six telephone EFT sessions, but 91% recover after in-person EFT sessions, showing that the latter are significantly more effective (Hartung & Stein, 2012). The work of licensed mental health professionals was compared to EFT delivered by life coaches and found to be slightly more effective (Stein & Brooks, 2011). Pain, depression, and anxiety all improved when PTSD was healed (Church, 2014). In tandem with PTSD, symptoms of TBI (traumatic brain injury) dropped by an average of 41% even though TBI was not the target of treatment (Church & Palmer-Hoffman, 2014).

In addition to these RCTs, there have been several studies in which EFT was used with groups of traumatized people. Their symptom levels were measured before and after treatment, rather than comparing them to a second group. Though not as strong evidence as RCTs, these studies nevertheless show the difference in the PTSD symptoms of sufferers before and after treatment.

In a pilot study of 11 veterans and family members at a 5-day retreat, they showed significant drops in PTSD symptoms (Church, 2010). Another pilot study was the precursor to the RCT summarized previously, and it was there that six sessions of EFT were found to permanently reduce PTSD symptoms in veterans (Church, Geronilla, & Dinter, 2009).

One large-scale study looked at the PTSD levels of 218 veterans and their spouses before and after attending a healing retreat (Church & Brooks, 2014). As part of the program they received 4 mornings of EFT. Each retreat lasted 7 days, and six retreats were conducted. They all showed the same pattern. An average of 82% of veterans had high or "clinical" PTSD symptom levels before the retreat; afterward, this number had dropped to just 28%. Additionally, 29% of the spouses also had PTSD going into the retreat, but only 4% afterward.

Another study offered 2 days of EFT training to 77 victims of the 2010 Haiti earthquake (Gurret, Caufour, Palmer-Hoffman, & Church, 2012). Before treatment, 62% of them tested positive for PTSD, while afterward 0% did. These studies show that EFT is effective when delivered in groups, as well as in individual counseling sessions.

Applying EFT

Now that you understand that Clinical EFT is an "evidence-based" practice, and that it is supported by a strong research base, in the rest of the book I'm going to show you what the symptoms of PTSD look like and how you can address them with EFT. I'll show you how EFT is applied in the most desperate of traumatic events, such as war and natural disasters, as well as personal disasters such as auto accidents, assault, and child abuse.

I'll walk you through the neurological changes that occur in the brains of PTSD sufferers, so you can see how it's not just a psychological problem, but a physical one too. I'll encourage you with lots of stories by people who've healed from PTSD and by therapists and life coaches who worked with them. We'll explore the differences between working with PTSD and working with other mental health conditions.

By the time you've read this book you'll have a comprehensive picture of how to use EFT for PTSD, and what's happening in the body and mind when you tap. You'll also have become involved with the large community of people and resources committed to clearing the human suffering caused by the condition. You'll have a resource you can share with professionals such as your doctor or therapist, and will have experienced the healing possible with these methods. You'll join the thousands of others who are determined to bring EFT to millions of suffering people, and share the vision of a world in which PTSD is as archaic a disease as typhoid or cholera. You'll get a glimpse of the possibility of the end of PTSD, not just for you and your loved ones, but also for the whole world. Thanks for joining me on this amazing journey!

About Posttraumatic Stress Disorder

Pervasive Psychological Trauma

Psychological trauma is widespread. While news reports focus on the high levels of PTSD found in veterans, trauma is far more prevalent in the civilian population than most people realize. Since the wars in Iraq and Afghanistan began in 2001, far more Americans have died at the hands of family members than have been killed in the Middle East. Women are twice as likely to be victims of domestic violence than they are to get breast cancer (van der Kolk, 2014, p. 348).

Much of this violence affects children. According to a report by the U.S. Department of Health and Human Services, 60% of older children had witnessed or experienced victimization in the past year. Close to half had experienced physical assault, and 25% had witnessed domestic or community violence (U.S. Department of Health and Human Services, 2012). Twice as many children are killed by firearms as by cancer.

Incest, the sexual abuse of a child by a family member, was once thought to be uncommon. In 1975, an authoritative source, the *Comprehensive Textbook of Psychiatry,* concluded that, "incest is extremely rare, and does not occur in more than 1 out of 1.1 million people" (Freedman, Kaplan & Sadock, 1975). However, recent estimates are that one in 10 boys has been molested, and one in five girls, usually by a family member (Gorey & Leslie, 1997).

It can take a surprisingly "minor" negative experience to traumatize a child. In a series of studies called the Still Face Experiments, Harvard psychiatrist Edward Tronick examined the effect on a child of a parent's emotional withdrawal (Tronick, Als, Adamson, Wise, & Brazelton, 1979; Tronick, 1989). He instructed the mothers of young babies around 6 months old to keep their faces impassive instead of interacting with their babies.

Figure 1. The Still Face Experiments.

When the mothers maintained a still face for a short period, instead of the constant interplay of facial expressions that we unconsciously but continuously use for connection, the babies noticed immediately. If the babies failed to receive facial communication within a minute or two, they became increasingly agitated, then distressed, and finally began to flop around in uncontrolled desperation. While the mother did nothing to harm the baby, the mere withdrawal of connection was sufficient to produce extreme emotional distress.

The phenomenon is not just emotional, it's physiological too. When their emotions are disrupted, their bodies are disrupted as well. "Babies cannot regulate their own emotional states, much less the changes in heart rate, hormone levels, and nervous system activity that accompany emotions" (van der Kolk, 2014, p. 112). They are dependent on cues from the adults around them to produce this regulation. Bonding produces a steady heart rate and a low level of stress hormones. An interruption of connection with their caregivers produces spikes in stress hormones, as well as dysregulation of the nervous system and heart rhythm.

Tronick's work showed that it doesn't take being beaten or abused to affect a young child; the simple absence of emotionally reassuring cues from a caregiver can be traumatic. Sometimes people in my live EFT Level 1 and 2 workshops say, "I grew up in a pretty normal family, I had a happy childhood. So why am I so screwed up?" The answer is that it can take a surprisingly small disconnect from mother or father to upset a young child.

Attachment: Secure vs. Disorganized

Children whose needs are attended to by their caregivers develop what's called "secure attachment." Babies communicate their distress directly and immediately when they feel uncomfortable physical sensations such as being hungry, feeling upset, being wet, and feeling tired. When their cries are heard and their needs met, they associate the communication of their needs with getting them met. They learn that it's safe and natural to be tuned in to your body, and aware of your needs.

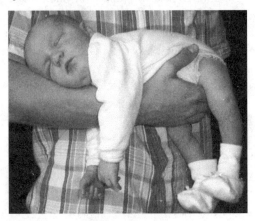

Figure 2. Secure attachment.

Children who don't receive consistent nurturing, or who are ignored or even abused, don't develop secure attachment. Instead they may become anxiously or ambivalently attached, as the parent from whom they're expecting care is unavailable or even a source of pain. They don't develop emotional or physical attunement with those around them, missing the cues that allow people to bond.

Children who are routinely abused or neglected can develop "disorganized attachment." They learn that their crying, pleading, and upset will not produce positive results from their caregiver. No amount of distress they exhibit in response to the physical and emotional signals they're getting from their body (hungry, tired, wet) is sufficient to get their needs met. The caregiver is not attuned to the baby's needs.

The child develops a "deep emotional learning" that his or her needs don't matter. The parent, for the baby the source of nurturing, is also the source of pain. For the baby, the parent is the source of survival, even if they're being abused. According to van der Kolk, "Terror increases the need for attachment, even if the source of the comfort is also the source of terror" (2014, p. 133).

When they're punished for simply expressing their needs, babies begin to associate having needs with pain. They shut down the impulses they're receiving from their bodies in an attempt to avoid punishment. They often develop a sense that there's something wrong with them. No amount of distress they express is enough to make the abuse stop. They become helpless in the face of abuse. This learning is taking place at a body level, long before they develop words, the ability to think consciously, and the brain structures required for cognitive interaction. This type of learning is occurring at the level of the cells, in the deepest layers of the body.

When their cries are heard and their needs met, babies develop a set of beliefs about the world and attitudes toward nurturing. The first way we learn about self-care is though the care we receive from others, which becomes the template for our subsequent worldview.

When children with disorganized attachment become adults, they may have little concept of self-care, and even become self-harming. They believe their needs don't matter, and that their existence is meaningless. They are chronically out of touch with their own bodies.

The Long-Term Results of Disorganized Attachment

The results of disorganized attachment and the dysfunctional lessons learned by such children show up in adulthood. In a 20-year longitudinal study of girls who had been sexually abused, the effects were found to be pervasive (Trickett, Noll, & Putnam, 2011). They had high levels of depression, obesity, dissociation, major illness, and self-mutilation. They entered puberty an average of 18 months earlier than non-abused girls. They had cognitive deficits and abnormal levels of certain hormones. Early in puberty, their levels of androstenedione and testosterone, hormones that stimulate libido, were three to five times higher. Their cortisol responses to stressful events were lower than normal, indicating that their bodies had adapted biochemically to high levels of emotional stress.

Another longitudinal study followed children for 30 years, all the way into adulthood (Sroufe, Egeland, Carlson, & Collins, 2010). It found the quality of early attachment to be the major predictor of adolescent and adult behavior. Children with disorganized attachment were chronically anxious. Not having learned the "dance of attunement" early in life, as adolescents they were unable to regulate their own emotions and had high levels of frustration, aggression, and disruptive behavior.

Figure 3. Traumatized child.

They exhibited a lack of empathy for the emotional distress of other people. They failed to develop healthy relationships with peers, caregivers, and teachers. By late adolescence, half of the children in the study had been diagnosed with a mental health condition, and had low levels of resilience, the ability to bounce back after an adverse experience.

Trauma Is Physical as Well as Psychological

Psychological trauma is not a merely psychological problem; it affects the body at the most fundamental levels. The most basic need of any organism is survival. Other needs, such as digestion, reproduction, and self-actualization, cannot be met if the organism fails to survive. The survival mechanisms of our bodies resulted in the fight-flight-freeze response, and you'll be surprised at how many parts of your life and behavior are driven by this response.

Because survival is essential, when an animal is under threat, every other need and function is recruited to ensure survival. Those physical systems that can assist (such as circulation and respiration) have their functions altered to support survival. Those that are unable to assist (such as reproduction and digestion) are simply shut down. An immediate threat produces a radical reorganization of cellular resources down to the molecular level.

The body's survival functions are controlled by the autonomic nervous system (ANS). At the top of the spinal cord is the hindbrain, the pinnacle of the ANS. It handles all the functions a newborn baby can perform, including excretion, respiration, circulation, and digestion. It continues to perform these functions for adults without any conscious input from the rest of the brain. They happen automatically; for the fancy word "autonomic," you can substitute the straightforward word "automatic" since all these functions are taken care of in a healthy body automatically, without any necessity for conscious thought.

The ANS has two distinct parts: the sympathetic and the parasympathetic. The sympathetic nervous system (SNS) is responsible for handling stress, while the parasympathetic nervous system (PNS) is responsible for relaxation. When we're stressed, the sympathetic half of the ANS is dominant, and when we're relaxed, the parasympathetic part takes over.

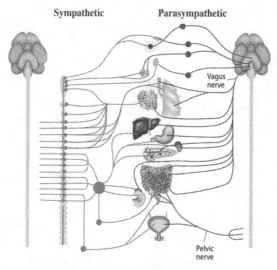

Figure 4. The sympathetic and the parasympathetic
nervous systems.

Take a look at the diagram of the sympathetic and parasympathetic systems (Fig. 4), and notice the radiating nerves. These nerves connect with your heart, your lungs, your eyes, your mouth, your digestive system, your liver, your bladder, and your reproductive organs. They're the conductor of the symphony, telling all the systems of your body what to do at any given moment. When you're relaxed, they sound the all-clear, and all your systems go into repair and rejuvenation mode. When you're stressed, they sound the alarm, and all your systems get ready for fight or flight. You can readily observe some of the organs regulated by the ANS when you reflect on the following types of events:

- You have to give a speech. Your mouth dries up. You have knots in your stomach.

- You remember the death of a loved one. You cry.

- You've been working on a project so intently that you forget everything else, and suddenly you're finished and you relax. You have to go to the bathroom.

- Your spouse brings up a dinnertime topic that upsets you. Your food curdles in your stomach.

- A person you despise enters the room. You bristle.

This stress-regulation system has worked so well, for so many millennia, that it's scarcely changed at all. The dinosaurs, extinct for 65 million years, had much the same ANS as you do. So do their descendants, today's lizards and birds. When you're a fetus growing in the womb, this part of your body develops first, just as it does in a salamander or an elephant. The reason that it's changed so little over millions of years is that it was perfected all those ages ago and it's simply so good at doing its job that Mother Nature has had no cause to tinker with it since.

Stress Is Hormonal as Well as Neurological

Neurotransmitters and hormones are molecules that work together with your ANS as a component of the system that signals your body to be stressed or relaxed. The two most important stress hormones are adrenaline and cortisol. Though there are others, I like to use cortisol as shorthand for the whole range of neurochemicals used in response to stress, because it can be measured in saliva and blood and there are many studies showing the stimuli that elevate its levels.

As a convenient shorthand for a relaxation hormone, I use DHEA (dehydroepiandrosterone), because it's your main relaxation hormone. Your body uses it for cell repair and rejuvenation, as well as signaling between cells. When you're stressed, your body makes more cortisol; when relaxed, more DHEA. These hormones move in concert with your SNS and PNS. When your SNS says go into flight or flight, you make lots of cortisol, and shut down production of DHEA. When your SNS says relax, you make lots of DHEA and reduce your production of cortisol. Understanding these cycles is vital to understanding your overall health because of all the body systems—digestion, circulation, reproduction, respiration,

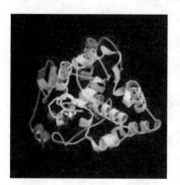

Figure 5. DHEA (l.) and cortisol (r.) molecules. Notice how similar the two molecules appear. That is because the body synthesizes them from the same precursors.

and immunity—that are affected by your level of stress and relaxation.

So if this system is so perfectly adapted to ensuring your survival, how can it be a problem? It's not a problem when children are raised with secure attachment, with periods of slightly elevated stress followed by relaxation and renewed attunement. The dance of attunement develops in the child a somatic or body-based sense of how to manage stress long before it develops the ability to think or reason. These abilities extend to its adult set of competencies.

When children are raised with disorganized attachment, however, they are in high stress mode most of the time. They live with their SNS on continual high alert. They adapt to having the neurophysiology of stress as their "set point." Stress is normal, while relaxation is not. As adults, they tend to have high levels of cortisol and low levels of DHEA. If they are highly stressed for long periods of time, they may deplete their stocks of both hormones, leading to the loss of energy characterized as "adrenal burnout." They may also develop abnormal patterns of cortisol secretion, such as low levels in the morning when cortisol is normally high to give you the energy to start your day, and high cortisol at night. This leads to insomnia and nightmares.

High stress is linked to virtually every type of disease. Studies show chronically high cortisol to be linked to loss of bone density, loss of muscle mass, increased skin wrinkling, cognitive decline, the inability to turn short-term into long-term memories, and many diseases.

While a cortisol spike is adaptive when it gives us the shot of juice required to evade danger, it takes a terrible toll on the body if the alarm system is turned on continuously. In traumatized people, it spikes higher and faster, and remains at a high level long after the danger has passed.

Your Body Can't Tell the Difference

Here's the real problem, and how this affects you whether you were raised with secure attachment, disorganized attachment, or anything in between: Your body can't tell the difference between a stressful thought and a stressful event. The subjective stressful thought that's "all in your mind" sends the same signal to your body that an actual objective threat to life and limb produces. Your cortisol shoots up within seconds. Your SNS goes into high alert. All your body systems are affected. You can do this by thought alone, without anything wrong in your environment. You've produced all the neurophysiology of

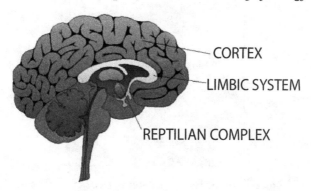

Figure 6. The triune brain.

stress in your body while having no objective reason to be on high alert.

The human brain has two layers above the reptilian survival system of the ANS. The midbrain or limbic system has many functions, and evolved later. It's the mammalian part of the brain, and it governs emotions. Mammals can feel emotionally in ways that reptiles cannot. They are able to navigate complex webs of social interaction. During the first 18 months after birth, the limbic system is the fastest-growing part of the brain, as the child is learning attachment and attunement. The lessons learned during this phase literally become part of the

Figure 7. Identifying threatening cues is essential to survival.

permanent wiring of the brain, which makes them so hard to change later in life.

Your midbrain also has two structures crucial to the emotional part of the stress response: the hippocampus and the amygdala. The hippocampus is like a military historian. Its job is to examine information coming in from the environment. If it finds a match between a piece of incoming information ("man wearing red shirt") and a previous threat ("I was beaten up when I was 7 by a bully in a red shirt"), it identifies a potential threat in the here and now.

The amygdala is like the fire alarm of the body. Once the hippocampus has made a positive match, and the match is confirmed by other structures in the brain, the amygdala's job is to sound the alarm, telling the SNS to go into fight-or-flight mode.

Driven to Distraction by Your Cortex

Above the mammalian brain is the primate brain, the cortex. This is the part of the brain that monkeys, dolphins, and other highly evolved species possess. It is largest in human beings, who have abilities that non-primates like dogs and cats do not. We're capable of abstract thought. We can reflect on the past, make projections about the future, and create highly structured mental products based on mathematics and poetry. We have language and song. All these are products of the cortex, which in evolutionary terms is the youngest part of the brain.

Where the cortex works against us is when we think abstract thoughts that drive strong emotion and trigger the fight-or-flight response. The thought, "John slammed my ideas at the staff meeting" isn't a threat to your survival, but if you're ruminating on it for hours over the weekend when you should be relaxing, you're driving your cortisol up and your DHEA down. You're engaging your SNS and negating all the cell repair and restoration processes governed by your PNS. There's no threat to your survival—the event happened several days before—yet you're still sending stress signals to your body.

The brain is constantly adding new connections, a process known as "neurogenesis." It's also pruning old unused circuits. While the ability of the brain to rewire itself in response to experience (this ability is called "neuroplasticity") is of great assistance when we're learning a new skill, it works against us when the circuits we're improving are those associated with stress. Stressed brains reinforce the neural pathways dedicated to carrying stress-related signals, at the expense of the brain regions responsible for memory, learning, and making high-quality executive decisions. Researchers have noted that PTSD symptoms often get worse over time, as neuroplasticity builds up the circuits of stress (Vasterling & Brewin, 2005). In an essay for the journal *Energy Psychology,* I call this "the dark side of neural plasticity" (Church, 2012).

Bringing the Traumatized Brain Back Online

The brains of people with PTSD do not process information as effectively as normal brains. The parts of the brain are unable to work in synchrony. Normally, all the regions of the brain work together when presented with incoming information. Figure 13 shows the difference (van der Kolk, 2014, p. 311). The PTSD brain has difficulty coordinating its activity in order to process the incoming information, and bring coherent focus to bear on the immediate situation.

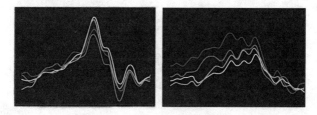

Figure 8. The brains of normal subjects coordinate their functioning to process information (left). The brains of PTSD sufferers aren't able to function in synchrony (right).

A team of EFT volunteers went to Haiti two years after the 2010 earthquake devastated the country and orphaned 250,000 children. They made a 7-minute video showing their work. You can see it at Haiti.EFTuniverse. com. One of the most touching scenes shows "Amelie," a girl who was 8 years old at the time of the earthquake. She and her mother were inside a building that collapsed. Her mother was killed, the girl survived, but it was two days before rescuers pulled Amelie from the rubble.

Imagine being trapped and immobilized with your mother's dead body for that length of time. Amelie was so traumatized that she had not spoken a single word in the two years since the earthquake. This is a classic example of the deactivation of Broca's area in the brain. She didn't socialize, laugh, or play with other children her age, indicating that her limbic brain was shut down.

Figure 9. Survivor of the 2010 earthquake in Haiti.

Under the guidance of the EFT practitioners, Amelie taps and starts telling a toy teddy bear how sad she is. After two days, the video shows her laughing and talking and playing with the other kids like a normal child of her age, as Amelie's entire brain comes back online and returns to synchrony.

In one large-scale study I performed with a group of colleagues, we analyzed the PTSD levels of 218 veterans and their spouses (Church & Brooks, 2014). Subjects attended one of six week-long retreats. Being married or coupled was one of the requirements of attendance. They did EFT for their PTSD symptoms in small groups. At the start of the retreats, 83% of the veterans met the criteria for a PTSD diagnosis. By the end, just 7 days later, only 28% did. When they were followed up 6 weeks later, they had maintained their gains (p < .001).

Living with a veteran with PTSD can by itself be traumatizing, and lead to "transferred PTSD." This phenomenon was evident in the spouses of the veterans in the study. When they began the retreat, 29% of the spouses also met the clinical criteria for PTSD. However, they had results similar to those of their partners. On follow-up, only 4% had diagnosable levels of PTSD. Each of the six retreats was analyzed separately, as though it were a small study by itself. The healing trajectory of participants was the same regardless of which retreat they attended, showing that the results were similar across the different groups. Being with a supportive partner can make a huge difference in the healing process. Social support reinforces the recovery of an individual.

Figure 10. Tapping session with a veteran.

While we might classify "physiological" or "medical" symptoms as a physical diagnosis, and "psychological" conditions such as phobias, depression, and PTSD as "mental" ones, they are often two sides of the same coin. Van der Kolk (2014, p. 188) notes that older WWII veterans are more comfortable couching their distress in terms of physical symptoms, while younger veterans of the recent Middle East wars are more comfortable describing their mental health challenges, but these are simply different frames of reference for the experience of traumatization.

Trauma that results from early childhood experiences with caregivers is harder to treat than trauma acquired in adulthood (van der Kolk, 2014, p. 210). For the veteran, the source of trauma is a clearly defined enemy. For the child, the source of trauma is a caregiver, a person who the child expects will nurture and care for them. This violation of expectations at a time when the brain is forming produces very deep emotional wounding. Van der Kolk calls this "developmental trauma," and argues that since it has unique characteristics, it should be included as a new diagnostic category in the DSM.

EFT is unique among therapeutic approaches in that it actually makes deliberate and systematic use of dissociation in the healing process. EFT recognizes that dissociation can perform a protective function. Chapter 6 describes EFT's three "Gentle Techniques" for working on events so traumatic they cannot be approached in ordinary states of consciousness. The three Gentle Techniques allow the client to dissociate just enough to feel safe, while also tapping. This creates enough psychological distance from the event to allow the client to begin the healing process. The felt sense of safety engendered by the Gentle Techniques quickly demonstrates to the client that it may be possible to reduce the degree of emotional triggering around the event. With this encouragement, the client then approaches the event at his or her own pace, dissociating less and less until he or she is able to tap on the memory itself without dissociation.

Stroking Your Inner Dog

Tapping on acupuncture points soothes the body. It sends a signal of safety to the emotional brain that counteracts the signal of stress coming from a traumatic memory. MRI studies show that acupuncture shuts down the brain's fear centers, regulating an overstimulated amygdala (Napadow et al., 2007; Hui et al., 2005; Fang et al., 2009). It speaks to the parts of the brain that respond to touch and other sensory input, not to the neocortex in which reason resides. For this reason I call it "stroking your inner dog."

Acupressure helps dissociated people feel safe in their bodies, sometimes for the first time. This provides them with a base of security from which they can begin the healing process, and start to unpack their trauma capsules. Randomized controlled trials show that as well as successfully treating PTSD symptoms in traumatized veterans, EFT reduces the symptoms of "somatization," the array of baffling physical ailments that have no medically discernible cause (Church, Hawk, et al., 2013; Geronilla, McWilliams, & Clond, 2014).

One of the three Gentle Techniques—Chasing the Pain—is specifically aimed at physical symptoms and is effective for clients who are uncomfortable talking about their emotions, but are very ready to describe their physical symptoms. Veterans in general and older veterans in particular are notoriously reluctant to discuss their mental health problems, but will readily describe physical symptoms: these are "medical" and "objective" and don't carry the perceived stigma that "emotional problems" do (van der Kolk, 2014, p. 19).

PTSD, Anxiety, and Depression as Chemical Imbalances in the Brain

Over the past century, physiologists have made many exciting discoveries about the body. The first hormone to be discovered was adrenaline (epinephrine) in 1900. In

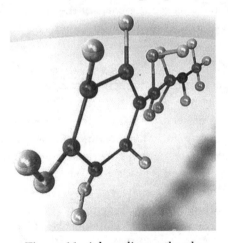

Figure 11. Adrenaline molecule.

1921, the first neurotransmitter, acetylcholine, was identified. As more of these essential protein molecules were discovered, and their link to human emotions understood, the race to find drugs that might modify their action began.

Pharmaceutical drugs have produced unparalleled improvements in human health in the past 150 years. Imagine a world before antibiotics or painkillers. However, because drugs have worked spectacularly well for certain conditions such as infectious diseases, the drug model has come to dominate medicine, displacing personal self-efficacy and non-pharmacological approaches such as psychotherapy and natural remedies.

My wife and I saw a 20-something woman tanning in the sun a few years back. "Aren't you afraid of skin cancer?" my wife asked her. She shrugged and said, "Soon the doctors will have a pill that will handle it." She was so confident in as-yet-undiscovered miracle cures that she was willing to bet her health on them, abdicating responsibility for her own well-being in the present, and handing it over to imaginary doctors of the future who would produce a magical cure for the results of her own self-neglect.

The biomedical model has come to dominate the popular imagination, as well as the professions of medicine and psychology. In the mid 20th century, psychotherapy was the way most mental illness was treated. Today psychotherapy has been displaced by drug therapies. Human brain function is regarded as a matter of chemistry rather than choice or behavior. A standard textbook declared: "The cause of mental illness is now considered an aberration of the brain, a chemical imbalance" (Deacon & Lickel, 2009).

However, the limits of this approach have become painfully obvious. Today prescription painkillers kill more people each year than guns or car accidents (van der Kolk, 2014, p. 349). While the cautious and appropriate prescribing of antidepressants and other psychotropic drugs can help certain patients, these drugs are being prescribed far more broadly than the scientific evidence supports.

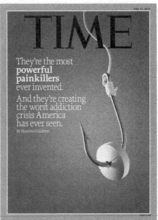

Figure 12. *Time* magazine—the painful cost of painkillers.

Because the number of prescriptions written for antidepressant drugs has soared, you would imagine that rates of depression should have plummeted. The opposite is true. The number of people diagnosed with depression has doubled in the past decade (Hidaka, 2012). In his book *Anatomy of an Epidemic*, medical journalist Robert

Whitaker outlines the research showing that many of these drugs have serious side effects, and that long-term use of antidepressants may actually cause chronic depression by disrupting the normal functioning of the brain (Whitaker, 2011).

The VA Could Have Remediated PTSD for Half the Cost of One Drug

During the first decade of this century, the U.S. Veterans Administration (VA) and the Department of Defense (DOD) spent $791 million on a drug called risperidone (Tal, 2013). Initially touted as a treatment for PTSD, a clinical trial published in the *Journal of the American Medical Association* eventually showed that it was no more effective than a placebo, an inert comparison pill (Krystal et al., 2011).

Because they offer the allure of a quick fix, writing prescriptions for PTSD and other mental health problems such as anxiety and depression has become the

Top drug sales

Top drug sales estimates for military and retail pharmacies, 2002-2011

Brand	Combined sales
Lipitor	$1,317,000,000
Plavix	$1,317,000,000
Advair	$1,148,000,000
Nexium	$983,000,000
Singulair	$973,000,000
Celebrex	$903,000,000
Zocor	$781,000,000
Prevacid	$670,000,000
Aciphex	$664,000,000
Actos	$613,000,000
Enbrel	$594,000,000
Effexor	$494,000,000
Fosamax	$481,000,000
Ambien	$417,000,000
Zyrtec	$413,000,000

Sources: TRICARE; Defense Logistics Agency

Figure 13. Military sales of top prescription drugs.

norm in the military. Meanwhile, the Pentagon and VA rebuffed repeated attempts to evaluate EFT, an evidence-based behavioral treatment, for PTSD. EFT studies were presented to the VA as early as 2008, when Senator Carl Levin, chair of the Senate Veterans Affairs Committee, wrote a personal letter to Secretary for Veterans Affairs Eric Shinseki, enclosing an early outcome study showing veterans recovering from PTSD after EFT treatment (Church, Geronilla, & Dinter, 2009).

Three other congressmen wrote to Shinseki again in 2010, enclosing more research and further evidence. They proposed seven simple and cost-free steps to help veterans gain access to EFT, such as circulating copies of clinical trials to VA mental health professionals. None of these steps was taken. In September 2013, Congressman Tim Ryan (D-Ohio) wrote another letter to Secretary Shinseki, this time advocating EFT on the basis of 11 clinical trials. Like all the other letters, this one was rebuffed, with the VA declining to examine the evidence, perform its own research, refer patients to the Veterans Stress Project, or take any other action to get EFT to suffering veterans.

The costs of such failure are staggering. Each veteran with PTSD costs an estimated $1.4 million to treat (Kanter, 2007). The cumulative cost to society of treating both the remaining 400,000 Vietnam veterans with PTSD, as well as the estimated 500,000 PTSD-afflicted veterans of the recent Middle East wars, exceeds $1 trillion (Church, 2014). By way of contrast, the cost of six sessions with an EFT practitioner for every one of these veterans comes to $300 million. For less than half of what the military spent on risperidone, it could have purchased this effective and safe behavioral treatment for every veteran with PTSD. If the results were as good as those in the studies, nearly nine out of 10 of those veterans would be PTSD-free today.

Meanwhile, the prescription drug machine rolls on. In 2012, according to an investigative report in the *American-Statesman,* "the Pentagon spent more on pills, injections and vaccines than it did on Black Hawk helicopters, Abrams tanks, Hercules C-130 cargo planes and Patriot missiles — combined" (Smith, 2012).

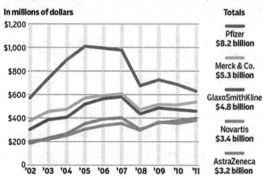

Military drug sales increase
Top 5 pharmaceutical companies sales estimates to the
Department of Defense, 2002-2011, based on retail and
military pharmacy sales. Excludes mail-order purchases.

In millions of dollars

	Totals
$1,200	Pfizer $8.2 billion
$1,000	Merck & Co. $5.3 billion
$800	GlaxoSmithKline $4.8 billion
$600	Novartis $3.4 billion
$400	AstraZeneca $3.2 billion
$200	
0 '02 '03 '04 '05 '06 '07 '08 '09 '10 '11	

In recent years prescription drug sales to the military have stabilized due
to a revamped formulary system, a push for beneficiaries to use less
expensive mail-order drugs, and rebates for retail pharmacy purchases.

Sources: TRICARE; Defense Logistics Agency   CHRISTOPHER SMITH / STAFF

Figure 14. Increasing revenue to Big Pharma from
military sales.

The widespread belief that there's a pill for everything leads both individuals and governments to seek medical solutions to problems instead of empowered personal action. Although our modern society has an impressive array of medical resources, they are not a substitute for self-care. Responsibility for our well-being rests on our own shoulders as individuals, and is not in the hands of our doctors and psychologists. They're there to support our health, not to magically fix us. Through practices such as yoga, mindfulness, relaxation, and EFT, we can regulate our own physiology, including neurotransmitters, hormones, genes and brain waves. No prescription is required.

When we practice responsible self-care, we're far less likely to require medical intervention. Postsurgical recovery times for fit and healthy people are much shorter. When we do have a crisis that requires medical intervention, we have a marvelous array of modern drugs and surgical techniques available to us, giving us the best of both worlds. Self-care and good medicine are both essential; neither excludes the other.

While working with WWII veterans with "shell shock," pioneering psychiatrist Joseph Wolpe discovered that diaphragmatic breathing was effective and developed the simple yet elegant scale that we use in EFT, called Subjective Units of Distress or SUD (Wolpe, 1958). People were instructed to rate their degree of emotional distress from 0, no distress, to 10, maximum possible distress, when remembering the event. A drop in the score meant that the treatment was succeeding.

Staying in the Body

Getting SUD scores every few minutes also encourages clients to stay tuned in to their bodies. Van der Kolk regards getting veterans "back into their bodies" to be one of the hallmarks of successful treatment (2014, p. 47). Another is bringing them back into the present moment. When they were traumatized, they learned how to escape the horror they were experiencing by dissociating, with awareness escaping from the here and now. Effective treatments put them back in touch with their physical sensations, and the reality of what's happening in the present.

Acupoint tapping wasn't practiced in the West during Wolpe's time, but EFT still uses the same SUD testing method, the same focus on the present moment, and the same body awareness. What Wolpe's diaphragmatic breathing and EFT have in common is that they keep the client from dissociating by maintaining a firm focus on the physical present. Other effective therapies such as Eye Movement Desensitization and Reprocessing (EMDR) and Somatic Experiencing do the same thing. They keep the client in the present moment, and in their body, while recalling a past trauma.

In all these therapeutic approaches, the immediate experience of physical safety effectively counterconditions the old stress response. Even though the traumatized person is thinking of a stressful event, these body-focused approaches remind them that they're safe in the here and now. This breaks the association in the brain's limbic system between the stressful memory and the fight-or-flight response. Once the association is broken one time, it's usually broken for good. That's why long-term studies that follow participants long after their EFT therapy sessions are over find that their recovery is permanent.

Talk therapy can be effective, and some approaches such as cognitive behavior therapy have a long track record of success. For traumatized people, however, talking about their issues can retraumatize them. In a large study of veterans diagnosed with PTSD and enrolled in a care program at a VA hospital, nine out of 10 did not complete the required program (Seal et al., 2010). We've heard this from many veterans who've been through our six-session EFT program at the Veterans Stress Project after dropping out of VA programs. They make statements like "Talking about the war just made me feel worse." In a study of cognitive behavioral therapy for PTSD, half the participants did not respond to treatment (Monson et al., 2006), in contrast to EFT studies that show upward of 80% veterans permanently rehabilitated.

Reducing Stress Hormones

In 2005, I had a striking experience while watching a group of trainee EFT practitioners. I was astonished at their incompetence. They were missing obvious physical cues from their clients, such as deep sighs and relaxing shoulders. They were missing verbal cues such as changes in psychological perspective, forgiveness, and acceptance. They didn't know the exact location of the acupressure points, and they were often tapping far off the mark. They were trying too hard to bring SUD scores down, instead of following and validating the client's experience. They were applying EFT techniques mechanically rather than organically. All of these mistakes were understandable on their learning curve.

What struck me forcibly, however, was that despite the shortcomings of the practitioners, the clients were getting results. They weren't getting results as good as they might have obtained from working with an expert practitioner, but they were getting results far better than those I'd seen in my earlier training in Gestalt therapy.

As I watched clients physically relax, I wondered what might be happening invisibly inside their bodies to their stress hormones. To answer this research question, I designed a study to examine their cortisol levels. With colleagues from the California Pacific Medical Center and the University of Arizona, I conducted the first study that examined both psychological conditions such as anxiety and depression, and cortisol levels before and after EFT (Church, Yount, & Brooks, 2012).

The study was ambitious and took several years to complete. It was conducted at five integrative medical clinics in California, and eventually included 83 subjects. It was a triple-blind randomized controlled trial, the highest standard of scientific proof. The results were remarkable, and the study was published in a prestigious journal, the oldest peer-reviewed psychiatry journal in North America.

We assessed subjects' mental health, and also measured their cortisol, before and after a single therapy session. One group received EFT, a second group talk therapy, and a third group simply rested. Psychological symptoms such as anxiety and depression declined in the talk therapy and rest groups, but they dropped more than twice as much in the EFT group. Cortisol dropped quickly and significantly. The study showed that EFT was having an effect inside the body.

Regulating Gene Expression

With some of the same colleagues, I began a randomized controlled trial examining changes in gene expression in veterans after 10 EFT sessions (Church, Yount, Rachlin, Fox, & Nelms, 2015). Again, the study was difficult to fund and accomplish, and took many years to complete. But the results were worthwhile, and echoed the physical effects we'd identified in the cortisol study. We found that genes associated with inflammation in the body were downregulated, like turning down the dimmer switch on a lamp. Genes associated with immunity were upregulated, or turned up. The psychological symptoms of PTSD dropped by over 50%, echoing the results of earlier studies (Church, Hawk, et al., 2013; Geronilla, McWilliams, & Clond, 2014). This study shows that EFT is an epigenetic intervention, affecting the body at the most basic level of molecular biology, the DNA.

Many studies have now linked emotional nurturing to gene expression. Stress-regulation genes are turned on in the brains of newborn rats that are attentively licked and groomed by their mothers (Bagot, et al., 2012). When the brains of schizophrenics who have committed suicide are compared with the brains of mentally healthy people who died in accidents, the genes responsible for regulating stress are found to be turned off. The DNA is still there, but it's been inactivated by the stressful experiences of early childhood (Poulter et al., 2008; McGowan et al., 2008).

The link between physical and emotional symptoms has been understood for over a century. In his book *The Traumatic Neuroses of War,* psychiatrist Abram Kardiner (1941) described his observations of WWI veterans. Even people who had been highly functional before the war became detached (dissociated) and hypervigilant. He understood that PTSD is a condition of the body as much as the mind, writing that the "nucleus," or center of traumatic stress was a "physioneurosis" that took root in the body. Though science in Kardiner's time knew nothing of gene regulation, the physical basis of PTSD was observed by him and many other clinical professionals treating veterans and other traumatized populations.

Eye Movements Link Brain and Body

Another compelling link between brain and body was discovered after WWII. A British ophthalmologist published a book in which he noted that veterans had erratic eye movements (Traquair, 1944). A study confirming the link between eye movements and PTSD involved a collaboration between a psychiatrist and an ophthalmologist checking refs (Tym, Beaumont, & Lioulios, 2009). They studied 100 patients, and found that those with PTSD had persistent difficulty maintaining the stability of their peripheral vision while contemplating a traumatic event.

After successful psychiatric treatment, however, the eye fluttering disappeared, and they were able to recall the event without either emotional distress or visual impairment. According to another published report, 90% of psychiatric patients have these visual anomalies (Tym, Dyck, & McGrath, 2000).

Neuroscientists don't know exactly why this association between traumatic memories and eye movements occurs. It may be linked to the ability of the brain to process a disturbing event. The limbic system contains structures that are responsible for turning short-term memories into long-term ones. This memory processing function is impaired in patients suffering from PTSD. This theory is discussed in an article in Scientific American (Rodriguez, 2012). It summarizes how research into EMDR, a therapy that is as effective as EFT for PTSD (Karatzias et al., 2011), demonstrates that the eye movements are an active ingredient of the therapy and not an inert placebo (Shapiro, 1989).

EFT uses a protocol for eye movements called the 9 Gamut Procedure (Callahan, 1985). It involves 9 actions performed while tapping a point called the "Gamut" point located on the Triple Warmer acupuncture meridian on the back of the hand. It includes eye movements, tapping, humming, and counting. The client moves his or her eyes slowly around a big circle at the extreme periphery of vision. The 9 Gamut Procedure is believed to engage parts of the brain involved in the nonverbal resolution of trauma. Other Clinical EFT Techniques such as the Floor to Ceiling Eye Roll (Feldenkrais, 1984) also use eye movements to reduce emotional distress. The developers of neuro-linguistic programming (NLP) believed that lateral eye movements correlate with aspects of experience such as internal dialog, kinesthetic sensations, and imagery (Bandler & Grinder, 1979). States such as REM sleep when the dreaming brain is in theta mode demonstrate that eye movements are part of the way the brain processes information.

I use the 9 Gamut Procedure often during live coaching calls. While most EFT techniques focus on neutralizing particular traumatizing events, the 9 Gamut Procedure is effective at neutralizing a whole class of events simultaneously. If I'm working with a man whose father beat him often as a child, I'll use this technique on all the beatings instead of focusing on a particular beating. If I'm working with a woman who was sexually molested as a child, I'll use the 9 Gamut on the group of adverse experiences rather than identifying particular events. Usually, the SUD score of such clients for the entire class of events drops slowly over the course of half an hour. This approach is much more efficient than working on the events one by one. Once you're finished with the 9 Gamut, you can test the effect of your work by having the client focus on a single event and determining whether it's been neutralized.

When I'm working with clients in workshops, I watch their eyes closely. The erratic peripheral vision movements noted by Traquair are readily observable by the coach (though not by the client). Frequently clients will move their eyes through every quadrant of the visual field except for one. They will consistently skip the same quadrant, like the hands of a clock going smoothly all the way around the face, but skipping between 3 and 6 o'clock. Once EFT has decreased the degree of distress, they no longer skip that quadrant, and their eye movements are smooth all the way around the field of peripheral vision.

Clinical experience by thousands of EFT practitioners working with tens of thousands of clients has shown the 9 Gamut Procedure to be effective even when the other parts of EFT's Basic Recipe are unable to provide resolution to a problem. While the cognitive parts of EFT may reach the reasoning brain operating in an alpha-beta mode, it's likely that the 9 Gamut technique is reaching the nonverbal and preverbal parts of the brain. These are operating in that theta-delta superlearning trance. Clients receiving a long and thorough session with eye movements appear to go into a trance state. The practitioner then introduces Reminder Phrases from the traumatic memory. While these might produce high emotion before treatment, these triggers are removed by the 9 Gamut. The client still has the memory, but it no longer evokes strong emotion. In this way the 9 Gamut is able to treat memory tracks laid down in a preverbal state early in childhood, as well as those produced by severely traumatic adult experiences.

Memory Reconsolidation and Extinction

Until the early 2000s, the prevailing view in neuroscience was that, once an experience had been installed in long-term memory, it was difficult or impossible to change (Ecker, Ticic, & Hulley, 2012). Beliefs about the self and the world formed in early childhood through strong negative emotional associations were "locked into the brain by extraordinary durable synapses" (Ecker et al., p 3). They were believed to persist throughout the person's entire life. These memories were said to be "consolidated" into the neural network.

Then a series of studies with animals showed that, under certain conditions, even long-consolidated memories might become "labile," or malleable, and susceptible to change. This led to the discovery that "a consolidated memory can return…to a labile, sensitive state—in which it can be modified, strengthened, changed or even erased!" (Nader, 2003, p. 65). Clinicians began to ask if this model might be applied to psychology, allowing, for instance, PTSD patients to undo the strongly conditioned and consolidated memories that had traumatized them so deeply.

Certain treatment sequences seem to allow the brain to revise even long-consolidated beliefs. These protocols have now been precisely delineated. Ecker, Ticic, &

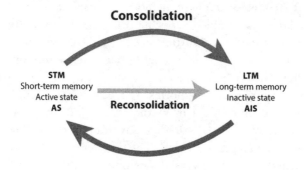

Figure 15. Memory reconsolidation.

Hulley (2012) call this the "transformation sequence," and break it into three interrelated stages:

1. Vivid re-exposure to the memory or experience must occur.

2. At the same time, a contradictory experience or memory ("juxtaposition experience") must be activated.

3. Several repetitions of the juxtaposition experience may be necessary in order for the new worldview to overwrite the old one.

Whether or not a therapist is aware of these three steps, Ecker and colleagues (2012) believe they are present in every successful therapeutic encounter. For this reason, Ecker calls this model a "meta-conceptualization" that applies to any type of therapy, not just to one school or technique.

Death in Vietnam: Joe's Story

A striking example of memory reconsolidation comes from "Joe," a disabled veteran with PTSD and multiple physical symptoms. During one the six free sessions he received from his EFT practitioner after enrolling in the Veteran's Stress Project, Joe shared one of his most disturbing intrusive memories. His best friend, Ted, had been killed by a sniper in Vietnam. Ted and Joe used to go on patrol each day. Joe usually walked on the right, while Ted walked on the left. The day Ted was shot, they happened to have reversed positions, with Joe on the left. For over 40 years, Joe had suffered from "survivor's guilt," and his narrative about the event was "The bullet was meant for me."

After tapping as he described each component of the memory, Joe had a sudden cognitive shift, saying, "I'm realizing that, like I would have died for him, Ted would have died for me. He would have wanted to take the bullet for me, just like I thought I should have taken the bullet for him." This new narrative led Joe to feel a sense of resolution around the event, and he was no longer troubled by it. His SUD score went to 0.

How EFT Applies the Three-Step Formula

In Step 1 of the formula identified by Ecker and colleagues (2012), Joe vividly recalled all the details of that day. EFT uses a Setup Statement to focus the client on the traumatic event, and a Reminder Phrase to keep attention on the event. Not only is the whole event recalled; Clinical EFT practitioners are trained to focus the client on all the details of the event, as well as sensory input that might be encoded in the trauma capsule. They might ask the client, "What did you see… taste… feel… touch… smell." An expert practitioner will mine the details of the event for every channel in which trauma might be encoded.

In Step 2, a contradictory experience is introduced in the form of tapping on acupoints. The soothing experience of tapping is juxtaposed with the upsetting memory being vividly recalled. The 9 Gamut Procedure may be added to the protocol. Limbic deactivation is occurring, PTSD-linked genes are being downregulated, and cortisol

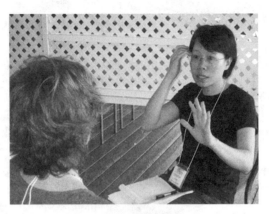

Figure 16. EFT session.

is being lowered, at the same time that the traumatic event is being held in memory.

In Step 3, repetition, the client taps repeatedly till the SUD score is reduced. This may take more than one round of EFT tapping. If the SUD level is not down to 0 after the first round, repeated rounds are performed. The 9 Gamut may be performed until the client's eyes are able to move smoothly through every degree of the peripheral visual field. The practitioner may dig for further details, and often clients access memory fragments they had forgotten or dissociated from before. An experienced Clinical EFT practitioner will keep asking questions until it is apparent that all the details and manifestations of the trauma have been extinguished.

At that point, the practitioner might instruct the client to make the details even more vivid or dramatic, in an effort to determine if the emotional charge of the memory has truly been extinguished. Once the client reports a

SUD score of 0 for even the most troubling aspects of the memory, and can later recall the memory while remaining at a 0 SUD level, the work of memory reconsolidation and extinction is done.

These memories are not "extinguished" in the sense of being erased. What is extinguished is the emotional distress associated with the memory. This can be tested days, weeks, or months after the event by asking the client to remember the event again. The memory is usually still intact but without the emotional charge. The client may evidence a cognitive shift with statements like "It was awful, but I grew stronger through the experience" or "My dad was abused by his dad much worse than he abused me." Cognitive shifts might take the form of changes in visual perspective. The person might now perceive themselves as witnessing the event rather than being part of the scene. The event may come into sharp focus. Or the opposite may happen, with a previously clear image now becoming blurry.

In this way, EFT is a short and efficient therapy for producing memory reconsolidation and the extinction of emotional cues, even in extreme trauma cases such as those resulting from the earthquake in Haiti and the genocide in Rwanda, and long-standing PTSD such as that found in Vietnam veterans. Feinstein (2010), reviewing eight studies examining the effect of acupoint tapping on PTSD, maintains that: "(a) tapping on selected acupoints (b) during imaginal exposure (c) quickly and permanently reduces maladaptive fear responses to traumatic memories and related cues."

The Future of Psychology and Medicine

I believe we are entering a new era in psychology and medicine as dramatic as the elimination of most infectious diseases at the start of the 20th century. Research shows that body-based approaches such as EFT and EMDR have the ability to remediate most mental health conditions in just a few sessions. Treatment time frames range from one session for phobias (Wells, Polglase, Andrews, Carrington, & Baker, 2003) to 10 sessions for difficult diagnoses such as PTSD (Church, Yount, Rachlin, Fox, & Nelms, 2015).

Figure 17. EFT session.

Imagine these therapies being available as front-line medical care. Imagine every veteran having access to EFT, and international initiatives to offer EFT to large groups of traumatized people. Imagine a society as dedicated to eliminating these mental health problems as we were to eliminating infectious disease. Imagine depression, anxiety, phobias and PTSD becoming as rare as polio, cholera, or typhoid fever. The infectious disease revolution was accomplished quickly, and the mental health revolution might occur just as quickly.

Imagine if future generations of children are raised by parents who have healed their own traumatic histories. Imagine if every child with test anxiety, social phobia, or public speaking anxiety had the tools of energy psychology at his or her fingertips. Imagine teams of mental health professionals treating survivors of natural and human-caused disasters, alleviating the suffering that would otherwise occur.

This is all very possible. As a society, we now have the tools to accomplish this, just as we accomplished the eradication of many infectious diseases generations ago. Having the tools, we now need the vision and the will to use them effectively. I believe that collectively we may well make this decision, resulting in a future society very different than the one we live in today. As we tap away our own individual traumatization, we will enjoy happier and more balanced lives. As we offer these methods to others, we contribute to a happier and more balanced society. Our children and grandchildren will thank us, just as we thank the heroes who gave us a world free of most of the diseases from which previous generations suffered. We are part of a large social movement that I believe will result in a future very much better than our past.

How to Do EFT:
The Basic Recipe

Over the past decade, EFT has been the focus of a great deal of research. This has resulted in more than 20 clinical trials, in which EFT has been demonstrated to reduce a wide variety of symptoms. These include pain, skin rashes, fibromyalgia, depression, anxiety, and post-traumatic stress disorder (PTSD). Most of these studies have used the standardized form of EFT found in *The EFT Manual.* In this chapter, my goal is to show you how to unlock EFT's healing benefits in whatever physical or psychological problems you're facing. I have a passionate interest in relieving human suffering. When you study EFT, you quickly realize how much suffering can be alleviated with the help of this extraordinary healing tool. I'd like to place the full power of that tool in your hands, so that you can live the happiest, healthiest, and most abundant life possible.

If you go on YouTube or do a Google search, you will find thousands of websites and videos about EFT. The quality of the EFT information you'll find through these sources varies widely, however. Certified practitioners trained in EFT provide a small portion of the information. Most of it consists of personal testimonials by untrained enthusiasts. It's great that EFT works to some degree for virtually anyone. To get the most out of EFT and unlock its full potential, however, it's essential that you learn the form of EFT that's been proven in so many clinical trials: Clinical EFT.

Every year in EFT Universe workshops, we get many people who tell us variations of the same story: "I saw a video on YouTube, tapped along, and got amazing results the first few times. Then it seemed to stop working." The reason for this is that a superficial application of EFT can indeed work wonders. To unleash the full power of EFT, however, requires learning the standardized form we call Clinical EFT, which has been validated, over and over again, by high-quality research, and is taught systematically, step by step, by top experts, in EFT workshops.

Why is EFT able to produce beneficial results with so many problems, both psychological and physical? The reason for its effectiveness is that it reduces stress, and stress is a component of many problems. In EFT research on pain, for instance, we find that pain decreases by an average of 68% with EFT (Church & Brooks, 2010). That's an impressive two-thirds drop. Now ask yourself, if EFT can produce a two-thirds drop in pain, why can't it produce a 100% drop? I pondered this question myself, and I asked many therapists and doctors for their theories as to why this might be so.

The consensus is that the two thirds of pain reduced by EFT is due largely to emotional causes, while the remaining one third of the pain has a physical derivation. A man I'll call "John" volunteered for a demonstration at an EFT introductory evening at which I presented. He was on crutches, and told us he had a broken leg as a result of a car accident. On a scale of 0 to 10, with 0 being no pain, and 10 being maximum pain, he rated his pain as an 8. The accident had occurred 2 weeks earlier. My logical scientific brain didn't think EFT would work for John, because his pain was purely physical. I tapped with him anyway. At the end of our session, which lasted less than 15 minutes, his pain was down to a 2. I hadn't tapped on the actual pain with John at all, but rather on all the emotional components of the auto accident.

There were many such components. His wife had urged him to drive to an event, but he didn't want to go and felt resentment toward his wife. That's emotional. He was angry at the driver of the other car. That's emotional. He was mad at himself for abandoning his own needs by driving to an event he didn't want to attend. That's emotional. He was upset that now, as an adult, he was reenacting the abandonment by his mother that he had experienced as a child. That's emotional. He was still hurt by an incident that occurred when he was 5 years old, when his mother was supposed to pick him up from a friend's birthday party and forgot because she was socializing with her friends and drinking. That's emotional.

Do you see the pattern here? We're working on a host of problems that are emotional, yet interwoven with the pain. The physical pain is overlaid with a matrix of emotional issues, like self-neglect, abandonment, anger, and frustration, which, in John's case, were part of the fabric of his life.

John's story has a happy ending. After we'd tapped on each of the emotional components of his pain, the physical pain in his broken leg went down to a 2. That pain rating revealed the extent of the physical component of John's problem. Two of the original eight rating points were physical. The other six points were emotional.

The same is true for the person who's afraid of public speaking, who has a spider phobia, who's suffering from a physical ailment, who's feeling trapped in his job, who's unhappy with her husband, who's in conflict with those around him. That is, all of these problems have a large component of unfinished emotional business from the past. When you neutralize the underlying emotional issues with EFT, what remains is the real problem, which is often far smaller than you imagine.

Though I present at few conferences nowadays because of other demands on my time, I used to present at about 30 medical and psychological conferences each year, speaking about research and teaching EFT. I presented to thousands of medical professionals during that period. One of my favorite sayings was "Don't medicalize emotional problems. And don't emotionalize medical problems." When I would say this to a roomful of physicians, they would nod their heads in unison. The medical profession as a whole is very aware of the emotional component of disease.

If you have a real medical problem, you need good medical care. No ifs, ands, or buts. If you have an emotional problem, you need EFT. Most problems are a mixture of both. That's why I urge you to work on the emotional component with EFT and other safe and non-invasive behavioral methods, and to get the best possible medical care for the physical component of your problem. Talk to your doctor about this; virtually every physician will be supportive of you bolstering your medical treatment with emotional catharsis.

When you feel better emotionally, a host of positive changes also occur in your energy system. When you feel worse, your energy system follows. Several researchers have hooked people up to electroencephalographs (EEGs), and taken EEG readings of the electrical energy in their brains before and after EFT. These studies show that when subjects are asked to recall a traumatic event, their patterns of brain-wave activity change. The brain-wave frequencies associated with stress, and activation of the fight-or-flight response, dominate their EEG readings. After successful treatment, the brain waves shown on their EEG readings are those that characterize relaxation (Lambrou, Pratt, & Chevalier, 2003; Swingle, Pulos, & Swingle, 2004; Diepold & Goldstein, 2008).

Other research has shown similar results from acupuncture (Vickers et al., 2012). The theory behind acupuncture is that our body's energy flows in 12 channels called meridians. When that energy is blocked, physical or psychological distress occurs. The use of acupuncture needles, or acupressure with the fingertips, is believed to release those energy blocks. EFT has you tap with your fingertips on the end points of those meridians; that's why EFT is sometimes referred to as "emotional acupuncture." When your energy is balanced and flowing, whether it's the brain-wave energy picked up by the EEG or the meridian energy described in acupuncture, you feel better. That's another reason why EFT works well for many different kinds of problem.

EFT is rooted in sound science, and this chapter is devoted to showing you how to do Clinical EFT yourself so you can enjoy some of the benefits research has demonstrated. It will introduce you to the basic concepts that amplify the power of EFT, and steer you clear of the most common pitfalls that prevent people from making progress with EFT. The basics of EFT, called the "Basic Recipe," are easy to learn and use. The second half of this chapter shows you how to apply the Basic Recipe for maximum effect and introduces you to all of the key concepts of Clinical EFT.

Testing

EFT doesn't just hope to be effective. We test our results constantly, to determine if the course we're taking is truly making us feel better. The basic scale we use for testing was developed by a famous psychiatrist, Joseph Wolpe, in the 1950s, and measures a person's degree of discomfort on a scale of 0 through 10. Zero indicates no discomfort, and 10 is the maximum possible distress. This scale works equally well for psychological problems such as anxiety and physical problems such as pain.

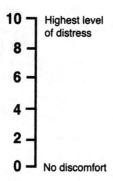

SUD scale (intensity meter).

Dr. Wolpe called this rating the SUD or Subjective Units of Discomfort. It's also sometimes called the Subjective Units of Distress scale. You feel your problem, and give it a number rating on the SUD scale. It's vital to rate your SUD level as it is *right now*, not imagine what it might have been at the time in the past when the problematic event occurred. If you can't quickly identify a number, just take your best guess, and go from there.

I recommend you write down your initial SUD number. It's also worth noting *where in your body* the information on your SUD level is coming from. If you're working on a physical pain such as a headache, where in your head is the ache centered? If you're working on a traumatic emotional event, perhaps a car accident, where in your body is your reference point for your emotional distress? Do you feel it in your belly, your heart, your forehead? Write down the location on which your SUD rating is based.

A variation of the numeric scale is a visual scale. If you're working with a child who does not yet know how to count, for example, you can ask the child to spread his or her hands apart to indicate how big the problem is. Wide-open arms mean big, and hands close together mean small.

Whatever methods you use for testing, each round of EFT tapping usually begins with this type of assessment of the size of the problem. This allows us to determine whether or not our approach is working. After we've tested and written down our SUD level and body location, we move on to EFT's Basic Recipe. It has this name to indicate that EFT consists of certain ingredients, and if you want to be successful, you need to include them, just as you need to include all the ingredients in a recipe for chocolate chip cookies if you want your end product to be tasty.

Many years ago, I published a book by Wally Amos. Wally is better known as "Famous Amos" for his brand of chocolate chip cookies. One day I asked Wally, "Where did you get your recipe?" I thought he was going to tell me how he'd experimented with hundreds of variations to find the best possible combination of ingredients. I imagined Wally like Thomas Edison in his laboratory, obsessively combining pinches of this and smidgeons of that, year after year, in order to perfect the flavor of his cookies, the way Edison tried thousands of combinations before discovering the incandescent light bulb.

Wally's offhand response was "I used the recipe on the back of a pack of Toll House chocolate chips." Toll

House is one of the most popular brands, selling millions of packages each year, and the simple recipe is available to everyone. I was astonished, and laughed at how different the reality was from my imaginary picture of Wally as Edison. Yet the message is simple: Don't reinvent the wheel. If it works, it works. Toll House is so popular because their recipe works. Clinical EFT produces such good results because the Basic Recipe works. While a master chef might be experienced enough to produce exquisite variations, a beginner can bake excellent cookies, and get consistently great results, just by following the basic recipe. This chapter is designed to provide you with that simple yet reliable level of knowledge.

EFT's Basic Recipe omits a procedure that was part of the earliest forms of EFT, called the 9 Gamut Procedure. Though the 9 Gamut Procedure has great value for certain conditions, it isn't always necessary, so we leave it out. The version of EFT that includes it is called the Full Basic Recipe (see appendix).

The Setup Statement

The Setup Statement systematically "sets up" the problem you want to work on. Think about arranging dominoes in a line in the game of creating a chain reaction. Before you start the game, you set them up. The object of the game is to knock them down, just as EFT expects to knock down your SUD level, but to start with, you set up the pieces of the problem.

The Setup Statement has its roots in two schools of psychology. One is called cognitive therapy, and the other is called exposure therapy. Cognitive therapy considers the large realm of your cognitions—your thoughts, beliefs, ways of relating to others, and the mental frames through which you perceive the world and your experiences.

Exposure therapy is a successful branch of psychotherapy that vividly exposes you to your negative experiences. Rather than avoiding them, you're confronted by them, with the goal of breaking your conditioned fear response to the event.

We won't go deeper into these two forms of therapy now, but you'll later see how EFT's Setup Statement draws from cognitive and exposure approaches to form a powerful combination with acupressure or tapping.

Psychological Reversal

The term "Psychological Reversal" is taken from energy therapies. It refers to the concept that when your energies are blocked or reversed, you develop symptoms. If you put the batteries into a flashlight backward, with the positive end where the negative should be, the light won't shine. The human body also has a polarity (see illustration). A reversal of normal polarity will block the flow of energy through the body. In acupuncture, the goal of treatment is to remove obstructions, and to allow the free flow of energy through the 12 meridians. If reversal occurs, it impedes the healing process.

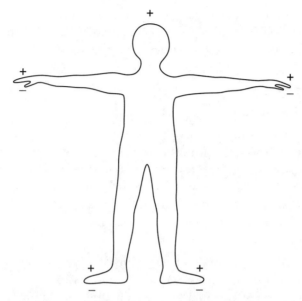

The human body's electrical polarity (adapted from
ACEP Certification Program Manual, 2006).

The way Psychological Reversal shows up in EFT and
other energy therapies is as a failure to make progress in
resolving the problem. It's especially prevalent in chronic
diseases, addictions, and conditions that resist healing. If
you run into a person who's desperate to recover, yet who
has had no success even with a wide variety of different
therapies, the chances are good that you're dealing with
Psychological Reversal. One of the first steps of EFT's
Basic Recipe is to correct for Psychological Reversal. It
only takes a few seconds, so we include this step whether
or not Psychological Reversal is present.

EFT's Setup includes stating an affirmation with those elements drawn from cognitive and exposure therapies, while at the same time correcting for Psychological Reversal.

Affirmation

The exposure part of the Setup Statement involves remembering the problem. You expose your mind repeatedly to the memory of the trauma. This is the opposite of what we normally do; we usually want an emotional trauma to fade away. We might engage in behaviors such as dissociation or avoidance so that we don't have to deal with unpleasant memories.

As you gain confidence with EFT, you'll find yourself becoming fearless when it comes to exposure. You'll discover you don't have to remain afraid of old traumatic memories; you have a tool that allows you to reduce their emotional intensity in minutes or even seconds. The usual pattern of running away from a problem is reversed. You feel confident running toward it, knowing that you'll quickly feel better.

The EFT Setup Statement is this:

Even though I have (name of problem), I deeply and completely accept myself.

You insert the name of the problem in the exposure half of the Setup Statement. Examples might be:

Even though I had that dreadful car crash, I deeply and completely accept myself.

Even though I have this migraine headache, I deeply and completely accept myself.

Even though I have this fear of heights, I deeply and completely accept myself.

Even though I have this pain in my knees, I deeply and completely accept myself.

Even though I had my buddy die in my arms in Iraq, I deeply and completely accept myself.

Even though I have this huge craving for whiskey, I deeply and completely accept myself.

Even though I have this fear of spiders, I deeply and completely accept myself.

Even though I have this urge to eat another cookie, I deeply and completely accept myself.

The list of variations is infinite. You can use this Setup Statement for anything that bothers you.

While exposure is represented by the first half of the Setup Statement, before the comma, cognitive work is done by the second half of the statement, the part that deals with self-acceptance. EFT doesn't try to induce you to positive thinking. You don't tell yourself that things will get better, or that you'll improve. You simply express the intention of accepting yourself just the way you are. You accept reality. Gestalt therapist Byron Katie (2002) wrote a book entitled *Loving What Is,* and that's exactly what EFT recommends you do.

The Serenity Prayer uses the same formula of acceptance, with the words, "God grant me the serenity to accept the things I cannot change; courage to change the things I can; and wisdom to know the difference." With EFT, you don't try and think positively. You don't try and change your attitude or circumstances; you simply affirm that you accept them. This cognitive frame of accepting what is opens the path to change in a profound way. It's also quite difficult to do this in our culture, which bombards us with positive thinking. Positive thinking actually gets in the way of healing in many cases, while acceptance provides us with a reality-based starting point congruent with our experience. The great 20th-century therapist Carl Rogers, who introduced client-centered therapy, said that the paradox of transformation is that change begins by accepting conditions exactly the way they are (Rogers, 1961).

I recommend that at first you use the Setup Statement exactly as I've taught it here. As you gain confidence, you can experiment with variations. The only requirement is that you include both a self-acceptance statement and exposure to the problem. For instance, you can invert the two halves of the formula, and put cognitive self-acceptance first, followed by exposure. Here are some examples:

I accept myself fully and completely, even with this miserable headache.

I deeply love myself, even though I have nightmares from that terrible car crash.

I hold myself in high esteem, even though I feel such pain from my divorce.

When you're doing EFT with children, you don't need an elaborate Setup Statement. You can have children use very simple self-acceptance phrases, like "I'm okay" or "I'm a great kid." Such a Setup Statement might look like this:

> *Even though Johnny hit me, I'm okay.*
>
> *The teacher was mean to me, but I'm still an amazing kid.*

You'll be surprised how quickly children respond to EFT. Their SUD levels usually drop so fast that adults have a difficult time accepting the shift. Although we haven't yet done the research to discover why children are so receptive to change, my hypothesis is that their behaviors haven't yet been cemented by years of conditioning. They've not yet woven a thick neural grid in their brains through repetitive thinking and behavior, so they can let go of negative emotions fast.

What do you do if your problem is self-acceptance itself? What if you believe you're unacceptable? What if you have low self-esteem, and the words "I deeply and completely accept myself" sound like a lie?

What EFT suggests you do in such a case is say the words anyway, even if you don't believe them. They will usually have some effect, even if at first you have difficulty with them. As you correct for Psychological Reversal in the way I will show you here, you will soon find yourself shifting from unbelief to belief that you are acceptable. You can say the affirmation aloud or silently. It carries more emotional energy if it is said emphatically or loudly, and imagined vividly.

Secondary Gain

While energy therapies use the term Psychological Reversal to indicate energy blocks to healing, there's an equivalent term drawn from psychology. That term is "secondary gain." It refers to the benefits of being sick. "Why would anyone want to be sick?" you might wonder. There are actually many reasons for keeping a mental or physical problem firmly in place.

Consider the case of a veteran with PTSD. He's suffering from flashbacks of scenes from Afghanistan where he witnessed death and suffering. He has nightmares, and never sleeps through the night. He's so disturbed that he cannot hold down a job or keep a relationship intact for long. Why would such a person not want to get better, considering the damage PTSD is doing to his life?

The reason might be that he's getting a disability check each month as a result of his condition. His income is dependent on having PTSD, and if he recovers, his main source of livelihood might disappear with it.

Another reason might be that he was deeply wounded by a divorce many years ago. He lost his house and children in the process. He's fearful of getting into another romantic relationship that is likely to end badly. PTSD gives him a reason to not try.

These are obvious examples of secondary gain. When we work with participants in EFT workshops, we uncover a wide variety of subtle reasons that stand in the way of healing. One woman had been trying to lose weight for 5 years and had failed at every diet she tried. Her secondary gain turned out to be freedom from unwanted attention by men.

Another woman, who suffered from fibromyalgia, discovered that her secret benefit from the disease was that she didn't have to visit relatives she didn't like. She had a ready excuse for avoiding social obligations. She also got sympathetic attention from her husband and children for her suffering. If she gave up her painful disease, she might lose a degree of affection from her family and have to resume seeing the relatives she detested.

Just like Psychological Reversal, secondary gain prevents us from making progress on our healing journey. Correcting for these hidden obstacles to success is one of the first elements in EFT's Basic Recipe.

How EFT Corrects for Psychological Reversal

The first tapping point we use in the EFT routine is called the Karate Chop point, because it's located on the fleshy outer portion of the hand, the part used in karate to deliver a blow. EFT has you tap the Karate Chop point with the tips of the four fingers of the opposite hand.

Karate Chop (KC) point.

Repeat your affirmation emphatically three times while tapping your Karate Chop point. You've now corrected for Psychological Reversal, and set up your energy system for the next part of EFT's Basic Recipe, the Sequence.

The Sequence

Next, you tap on meridian end points in sequence. Tap firmly, but not harshly, with the tips of your first two fingers, about seven times on each point. The exact number is not important; it can be a few more or less than seven. You can tap on either the right or left side of your body, with either your dominant or nondominant hand.

First tap on the meridian endpoints found on the face (see illustration). These are: (1) at the start of the eyebrow, where it joins the bridge of the nose; (2) on the outside edge of the eye socket; (3) on the bony ridge of the eye socket under the pupil; (4) under the nose; and (5) between the lower lip and the chin.

Then tap (6) on one of the collarbone points (see illustration). To locate this point, place a finger in the notch between your collarbones. Move your finger down about an inch and you'll feel a hollow in your breastbone. Now move it to the side about an inch and you'll find a deep hollow below your collarbone. You've now located the collarbone acupressure point.

Finally, tap (7) on the under the arm point, which is about four inches below the armpit (for women, this is where a bra strap crosses).

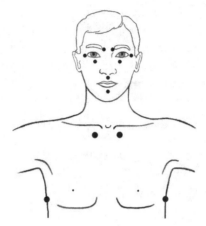

EB, SE, UE, UN, Ch, CB and UA points.

The Reminder Phrase

Earlier, I emphasized the importance of exposure. Exposure therapy has been the subject of much research, which has shown that prolonged exposure to a problem, when coupled with techniques to calm the body, treats traumatic stress effectively. EFT incorporates exposure in the form of a Reminder Phrase. This is a brief phrase that keeps the problem at the front of your mind while you tap on the acupressure points. It keeps your energy system focused on the specific issue you're working on, rather than jumping to other thoughts and feelings. The aim of the Reminder Phrase is to bring the problem vividly into your experience, even though the emotionally triggering situation might not be present now.

For instance, if you have test anxiety, you use the Reminder Phrase to keep you focused on the fear, even though you aren't actually taking a test right now. That gives EFT an opportunity to shift the pattern in the absence of the real problem. You can also use EFT during an actual situation, such as when you're taking an actual test, but most of the time you're working on troublesome memories. The Reminder Phrase keeps you targeted on the problem. An example of a Reminder Phrase for test anxiety might be *"That test"* or *"The test I have to take tomorrow"* or *"That test I failed."* Other examples of Reminder Phrases are:

The bee sting
Dad hit me
Friend doesn't respect me
Lawyer's office
Sister told me I was fat
Car crash
This knee pain

Tap each point while repeating your Reminder Phrase. Then tune in to the problem again, and get a second SUD rating. The chances are good that your SUD score will now be much lower than it was before.

These instructions might seem complicated the first time you read them, but you'll soon find you're able to complete a round of EFT tapping from memory in 1 to 2 minutes.

Let's now summarize the steps of EFT's Basic Recipe:

1. Assess your SUD level.

2. Insert the name of your problem into the Setup Statement: *"Even though I have (this problem), I deeply and completely accept myself."*

3. Tap continuously on the Karate Chop point while repeating the Setup Statement three times.

4. While repeating the Reminder Phrase, tap about seven times on the other seven points.

5. Test your results with a second SUD rating.

Isn't that simple? You now have a tool that, in just a minute or two, can effectively neutralize the emotional sting of old memories, as well as help you get through bad current situations. After a few rounds of tapping, you'll find you've effortlessly memorized the Basic Recipe, and you'll find yourself using it often in your daily life.

If Your SUD Level Doesn't Come Down to 0

Sometimes a single round of tapping brings your SUD score to 0. Sometimes it only brings it down slightly. Your migraine might have been an 8, and after a round of EFT it's a 4. In these cases, we do EFT again. You can adjust your affirmation to acknowledge that a portion of the problem sill remains, for example, *"Even though I still have some of this migraine, I deeply and completely accept myself."* Here are some further examples:

> *Even though I still feel some anger toward my friend for putting me down, I deeply and completely accept myself.*

> *Even though I still have a little twinge of that knee pain, I deeply and completely accept myself.*

Even though the bee sting still smarts slightly, I deeply and completely accept myself.

Even though I'm still harboring some resentment toward my boss, I deeply and completely accept myself.

Even though I'm still somewhat frustrated with my daughter for breaking her agreement, I deeply and completely accept myself.

Even though I'm still upset when I think of being shipped to Iraq, I deeply and completely accept myself.

Adjust the Reminder Phrase accordingly, as in *"some anger still"* or *"remaining frustration"* or *"bit of pain"* or *"somewhat upset."*

EFT for You and Others

You can do EFT on yourself, as you've experienced during these practice rounds. You can also tap on others. Many therapists, life coaches, and other practitioners offer EFT professionally to clients. I'm far more inclined to have clients tap on themselves during EFT sessions, even in the course of a therapy or coaching session. Though the coach can tap on the client, having clients tap on themselves, with some guidance by the coach, puts the power squarely in the clients' hands. Clients are empowered by discovering that they are able to reduce their own emotional distress, and they leave the practitioner's office with a self-help tool at their fingertips any time they need it. In some jurisdictions, it is illegal or unethical for therapists to touch clients at all, and EFT when done only by the client is still effective in these cases.

The Importance of Targeting Specific Events

During EFT workshops, I sometimes write on the board:

The Three Most Important Things About EFT

Then, under that, I write:

Specific Events
Specific Events
Specific Events

It's my way of driving home the point that a focus on specific events is critical to success in EFT. In order to release old patterns of emotion and behavior, it's vital to identify and correct the specific events that gave rise to those problems. When you hear people say, "I tried EFT and it didn't work," the chances are good that they were tapping on generalities, instead of specifics.

An example of a generality is "self-esteem" or "depression" or "performance problems." These aren't specific events. Beneath these generalities is a collection of specific events. The person with low self-esteem might have been coloring a picture at the age of 4 when her mother walked in and criticized her for drawing outside the lines. She might have had another experience of a schoolteacher scolding her for playing with her hair during class in second grade, and a third experience of her first boyfriend deciding to ask another girl to the school dance. Together, those specific events contributed to the global pattern of low self-esteem. The way EFT works is that when the emotional trauma of those individual events is resolved, the whole pattern of low self-esteem can shift. If you tap on the big pattern, and omit the specific events, you're likely to have limited success.

When you think about how a big pattern like low self-esteem is established, this makes sense. It's built up through many single events. Collectively, they form the whole pattern. The big pattern doesn't spring to life fully formed; it's built gradually out of many similar experiences. The memories engraved in your brain are of individual events; one disappointing or traumatic memory at a time is encoded in your memory bank. When enough similar memories have accumulated, their commonalities combine to create a common theme like "poor self-esteem." Yet the theme originated as a series of specific events, and that's where EFT can be effectively applied.

You don't have to use EFT on every single event that contributed to the global theme. Usually, once a few of the most disturbing memories have lost their emotional impact, the whole pattern disappears. Memories that are similar lose their impact once the most vivid memories have been neutralized with EFT.

Tapping on global issues is the single most common mistake newcomers make with EFT. Using lists of tapping phrases from a website or a book, or tapping on generalities, is far less effective than tuning in to the events that contributed to your global problem, and tapping on them. If you hear someone say, "EFT doesn't work," the chances are good they've been tapping globally rather than identifying specific events. Don't make this elementary mistake. List the events, one after the other, that stand out most vividly in your mind when you think about the global problem. Tap on each of them, and you'll usually find the global problem diminishing of its own accord. This is called the "generalization effect," and it's one of the key concepts in EFT.

Tapping on Aspects

EFT breaks traumatic events and other problems into smaller pieces called "aspects." The reason for this is that the highest emotional charge is typically found in one small chunk of the event, rather than the entirety of the event. You might need to identify several different aspects, and tap on each of them, before the intensity of the whole event is reduced to a 0.

Here's an example of tapping on aspects, drawn from experience at an EFT workshop I taught. A woman in her late 30s volunteered as a subject. She'd had neck pain and limited range of motion since an automobile accident 6 years before. She could turn her head to the right most of the way but had only a few degrees of movement to the left. The accident had been a minor one, and why she still suffered 6 years later was something of a mystery to her.

I asked her to feel where in her body she felt the most intensity when recalling the accident, and she said it was in her upper chest. I then asked her about the first time she'd ever felt that way, and she said it was when she'd been involved in another auto accident at the age of 8. Her sister had been driving the car. We worked on each aspect of the early accident. The two girls had hit another car head on at low speed while driving around a bend on a country road. One emotionally triggering aspect was the moment she realized that a collision was unavoidable, and we tapped till that lost its force. We tapped on the sound of the crash, another aspect. She had been taken to a neighbor's house, bleeding from a cut on her head, and we tapped on that. We tapped on aspect after aspect. Still, her pain level didn't go down much, and her range of motion didn't improve.

Then she gasped and said, "I just remembered. My sister was only 15 years old. She was underage. That day, I dared her to drive the family car, and we totaled it." Her guilt turned out to be the aspect that held the most emotional charge, and after we tapped on that, her pain disappeared, and she regained full range of motion in her neck. If we'd tapped on the later accident, or failed to uncover all the aspects, we might have thought, "EFT doesn't work."

Aspects can be pains, physical sensations, emotions, images, sounds, tastes, odors, fragments of an event, or beliefs. Make sure you dig deep for all the emotional charge held in each aspect of an event before you move on to the next one. One way of doing this is to check each sensory channel, and ask, "What did you hear/see/taste/touch/smell?" For one person, the burned-rubber smell of skidding tires might be the most terrifying aspect of a car accident. For another, it might be the smell of blood. Yet another person might remember most vividly the sound of the crash or the screams. For another person, the maximum emotional charge might be held in the feeling of terror at the moment of realization that the crash was inevitable. The pain itself might be an aspect. Guilt, or any other emotion, can be an aspect. For traumatic events, it's necessary to tap on each aspect.

Thorough exploration of all the aspects will usually yield a complete neutralization of the memory. If there's still some emotional charge left, the chances are good that you've missed an aspect, so go back and find out what shards of trauma might still be stuck in place.

Finding Core Issues

One of my favorite sayings during EFT workshops is "The problem is never the problem." What I mean by this is that the problem we complain about today usually bothers us only because it resembles an earlier problem. For example, if your spouse being late disturbs you, you may discover by digging deep with EFT that the real reason this behavior triggers you is that your mother didn't meet your needs in early childhood. Your spouse's behavior in the present day resembles, to your brain, the neglect you experienced in early childhood, so you react accordingly. You put a lot of energy into trying to change your spouse when the present-day person is not the source of the problem.

On the EFT Universe website, we have published hundreds of stories in which someone was no longer triggered by a present problem after the emotional charge was removed from a similar childhood event. Nothing changed in the present day, yet the very problem that so vexed a person before now carries zero emotional charge. That's the magic that happens once we neutralize core issues with EFT. Rather than being content with using EFT on surface problems, it's worth developing the skills to find and resolve the core issues that are at the root of the problem.

Here are some questions you might ask in order to identify core issues:

- Does the problem that's bothering you remind you of any events in your childhood? Tune in to your body and feel your feelings. Then travel back in time to the first time in your life you ever felt that same sensation.

- What's the worst similar experience you ever had?

- If you were writing your autobiography, what chapter would you prefer to delete, as though it had never happened to you?

If you can't remember a specific childhood event, simply make up a fictional event in your mind. This kind of guessing usually turns out to be right on target. You're assembling the imagined event out of components of real events, and the imaginary event usually leads back to actual events you can tap on. Even if it doesn't, and you tap on the fictional event, you will usually experience an obvious release of tension.

The Generalization Effect

The generalization effect is a phenomenon you'll notice as you make progress with EFT. As you resolve the emotional sting of specific events, other events with a similar emotional signature also decrease in intensity. I once worked with a man at an EFT workshop whose father had beaten him many times during his childhood. His SUD level on the beatings was a 10. I asked him to recall the worst beating he'd ever suffered. He told me that when he was 8 years old, his father had hit him so hard he had broken the boy's jaw. We tapped together on that terrible beating, and after working on all the aspects, his SUD score dropped to a 0. I asked him for a SUD rating on all the beatings, and his face softened. He said, "My dad got beat by his dad much worse than he beat me. My dad actually did a pretty good job considering how badly he was raised." My client's SUD level on all the beatings dropped considerably after we reduced the intensity of this one beating. That's an example of EFT's generalization effect. When you knock down an important domino, all the other dominoes can fall.

This is very reassuring to clients who suffered from many instances of childhood abuse, the way my client at that workshop had suffered. You don't need to work through every single horrible incident. Often, simply collapsing the emotional intensity behind one incident is sufficient to collapse the intensity around similar incidents.

The reason our brains work this way is because of a group of neurons in the emotional center of the brain (the limbic system) called the hippocampus. The hippocampus has the job of comparing one event to the other. Suppose that, as a 5-year-old child in Catholic school, you were beaten by a nun. Forty years later, you can't figure out why you feel uneasy around women wearing outfits that are black and white. The reason for your adult aversion to a black-and-white combination is that the hippocampus associates the colors of the nun's habit with the pain of the beating.

This was a brilliant evolutionary innovation for your ancestors. Perhaps these early humans were attacked by a tiger hiding in the long grass. The tiger's stripes mimicked the patterns of the grass, yet there was something different there. Learning to spot a pattern, judge the differences, and react with fear saved your alert ancestors. They gave birth to their children, who also learned, just a little bit better, how to respond to threats. After thousands of generations, you have a hippocampus at the center of your brain that is genetically engineered to evaluate every message flooding in from your senses, and pick out those associated with the possibility of danger. You see the woman wearing the black-and-white cocktail dress at a party, your hippocampus associates these colors with the nun who beat you, and you have an emotional response.

Yet the opposite is also true. Assume for a moment you're a man who is very shy when confronted with women at cocktail parties. He feels a rush of fear whenever he thinks about talking to an attractive woman dressed in black. He works with an EFT coach on his memories of getting beaten by the nun in Catholic school, and suddenly he finds himself able to talk easily to women at parties. Once the man's hippocampus breaks the connection between beatings and a black dress, it knows, for future reference, that the two phenomena are no longer connected. This is the explanation the latest brain science gives us for the generalization effect (Phelps & LeDoux,

2005). It's been noted in EFT for many years, and it's very comforting for those who've suffered many adverse experiences. You may need to tap on some of them, but you won't have to tap on all of them before the whole group is neutralized. Sometimes, like my client who was beaten repeatedly as a child, if you tap on a big one, the generalization effect reduces the emotional intensity of all similar experiences.

The Movie Technique and Tell the Story Technique

When you take an EFT workshop, the first key technique you learn is the Movie Technique. Why do we place such emphasis on the Movie Technique? The reason is that it combines many of the methods that are key to success with EFT.

The first thing the Movie Technique does is focus you on being specific. EFT is great at eliminating the emotional intensity you feel, as long as it's used on an actual concrete event ("John yelled at me in the meeting") rather than a general statement ("My procrastination").

The Movie Technique has you identify a particular incident that has a big emotional charge for you, and systematically reduce that charge to 0. You picture the event in your mind's eye as though it were a movie, and run through the movie scene by scene.

Whenever you reach a part of the movie that carries a big emotional charge, you stop and perform the EFT sequence. In this way, you reduce the intensity of each of the bad parts of the movie. EFT's related technique, Tell the Story, is done out loud, while the Movie Technique is typically done silently. You can use the Movie Technique with a client without the client ever disclosing what the event was.

Try this with one of your own traumatic life events right now. Think of the event as though it were a scary movie. Make sure it's an event that lasts just a few minutes; if your movie lasts several hours or days, you've probably picked a general pattern. Try again, selecting a different event, till you have a movie that's just a few minutes long.

One example is a man whose general issue is "Distrust of Strangers." We traced it to a particular childhood incident that occurred when the man, whom we'll call David, was 7 years old. His parents moved to a new town, and David found himself walking to a new school through a rough neighborhood. He encountered a group of bullies at school but always managed to avoid them. One day, walking back from school, he saw the bullies walking toward him. He crossed the street, hoping to avoid their attention. He wasn't successful, and he saw them point at him, then change course to intercept him. He knew he was due for a beating. They taunted him and shoved him, and he fell into the gutter. His mouth hit the pavement, and he chipped a tooth. Other kids gathered round and laughed at him, and the bullies moved off. He picked himself up and walked the rest of the way home.

If you were to apply EFT to David's general pattern, "Distrust of Strangers," you'd be tapping generally—and ineffectually. When instead you focus on the specific event, you're homing in on the life events that gave rise to the general pattern. A collection of events like David's beating can combine to create the general pattern.

Now give your movie a title. David might call his movie "The Bullies."

Start thinking about the movie at a point before the traumatic part began. For David, that would be when he was walking home from school, unaware of the events in store for him.

Now run your movie through your mind till the end. The end of the movie is usually a place where the bad events are over. For David, this might be when he picked himself up off the ground, and resumed his walk home.

Now let's add EFT to your movie. Here's the way you do this:

1. Think of the title of your movie. Rate the degree of your emotional distress around just the title, not the movie itself. For instance, on the distress scale of 0 to 10, where 0 is no distress and 10 represents maximum distress, you might be an 8 when you think of the title "The Meeting." Write down your movie title, and your number.

2. Work the movie title into an EFT Setup Statement. It might sound something like this: *"Even though I experienced [insert your movie title here], I deeply and completely accept myself."* Then tap on the EFT acupressure points, while repeating the Setup Statement three times. Your distress level will typically go down. You may have to do EFT several times on the title for it to reach a low number, 0 or 1 or 2.

3. Once the title reaches a low number, think of the "neutral point" before the bad events in the movie began to take place. For David, the neutral point was when he was walking home from school, before the bullies saw him. Once you've identified the neutral point of your own movie, start running the movie through your mind, until you reach a point where the emotional intensity rises. In David's case, the first emotionally intense point was when he saw the bullies.

4. Stop at this point, and assess your intensity number. It might have risen from a 1 to a 7, for instance. Then perform a round of EFT on that first emotional crescendo. For David, it might be, *"Even though I saw the bullies turn toward me, I deeply and completely accept myself."* Use the same kind of statement for your own problem: *"Even though [first emotional crescendo], I deeply and completely accept myself."* Keep tapping till your number drops to 0 or near 0, perhaps a 1 or 2.

5. Now rewind your mental movie to the neutral point, and start running it in your mind again. Stop at the first emotional crescendo. If you sail right through the first one you tapped on, you know you've really and truly resolved that aspect of the memory with EFT. Go on to the next crescendo. For David, this might have been when the bullies shoved him into the gutter. When you've found your second emotional crescendo, then repeat the process: Assess your intensity number, do EFT, and keep tapping till your num-

ber is low. Even if your number is only a 3 or 4, stop and do EFT again. Don't push through low-intensity emotional crescendos; since you have the gift of freedom at your fingertips, use it on each part of the movie.

6.   Rewind to the neutral point again, and repeat the process.

7.   When you can replay the whole movie in your mind, from the neutral point to the end of the movie when your feelings are neutral again, without feeling an emotional charge, you'll know you've resolved the whole event. You'll have dealt with all the aspects of the traumatic incident.

8.   To truly test yourself, run through the movie but exaggerate each sensory channel. Imagine the sights, sounds, smells, tastes, and other aspects of the movie as vividly as you possibly can. If you've been running the movie silently in your mind, speak it out loud. When you cannot possibly make yourself upset, you're sure to have resolved the lingering emotional impact of the event. The effect is usually permanent.

When you work through enough individual movies in this way, the whole general pattern often vanishes. Perhaps David had 40 events that contributed to his distrust of strangers. He might need to do the Movie Technique on all 40, but experience with EFT suggests that when you resolve just a few key events, perhaps 5 or 10 of them, the rest fade in intensity, and the general pattern itself is neutralized.

The Tell the Story Technique is similar to the Movie Technique; as mentioned, the Movie Technique is usually performed silently while Tell the Story is out loud. One great benefit of the Movie Technique done silently is that the client does not have to disclose the nature of the problem. An event might be too triggering, too embarrassing, or too emotionally overwhelming to be spoken aloud. That's no problem with the Movie Technique, which allows EFT to work its magic without the necessity of disclosure on the part of the client. The privacy offered by the Movie Technique makes it very useful for clients who would rather not talk openly about troubling events.

Constricted Breathing

Here's a way to demonstrate how EFT can affect you physically. You can try this yourself right now. It's often practiced as an onstage demonstration at EFT workshops. You simply take three deep breaths, stretching your lungs as far as they can expand. On the third breath, rate the extent of the expansion of your lungs on a 0-to-10 scale, with 0 being as constricted as possible, and 10 being as expanded as possible. Now perform several rounds of EFT using Setup Statements such as:

Even though my breathing is constricted...

Even though my lungs will only expand to an 8...

Even though I have this physical problem that prevents me breathing deeply...

Now take another deep breath and rate your level of expansion. Usually, there's substantial improvement.

Now focus on any emotional contributors to constricted breathing. Use questions like:

- What life events can I associate with breathing problems?

- Are there places in my life where I feel restricted?

- If I simply guess at an emotional reason for my constricted breathing, what might it be?

Now tap on any issues surfaced by these questions. After your intensity is reduced, take another deep breath and rate how far your lungs are now expanding. Even if you were a 10 earlier, you might now find you're an 11 or 14.

The Personal Peace Procedure

The Personal Peace Procedure consists of listing every specific troublesome event in your life and systematically using EFT to tap away the emotional impact of these events. With due diligence, you knock over every negative domino on your emotional playing board and, in so doing, remove significant sources of both emotional and physical ailments. You experience personal peace, which improves your work and home relationships, your health, and every other area of your life.

Tapping on large numbers of events one by one might seem like a daunting task, but we'll show you in the next few paragraphs how you can accomplish it quickly and efficiently. Because of EFT's generalization effect, where tapping on one issue reduces the intensity of similar issues, you'll typically find the process going much faster than you imagined.

Removing the emotional charge from your specific events results in less and less internal conflict. Less internal conflict results, in turn, in greater personal peace and less suffering on all levels—physical, mental, emotional, and spiritual. For many people, the Personal Peace Procedure has led to the complete cessation of lifelong issues that other methods did not resolve. You'll find stories on the EFT Universe website written by people who describe relief from physical maladies such as headaches, breathing difficulties, and digestive disorders. You'll read other stories of people who used EFT to help them deal with the stress associated with AIDS, multiple sclerosis, and cancer. Unresolved anger, trauma, guilt, or grief contributes to physical illness, and cannot be medicated away. EFT addresses these emotional contributors to physical disease.

Here's how to do the Personal Peace Procedure:

1. List every specific troublesome event in your life that you can remember. Write them down in a Personal Peace Procedure journal. "Troublesome" means it caused you some form of discomfort. If you listed fewer than 50 events, try harder to remember more. Many people find hundreds. Some bad events you recall may not seem to cause you any current discomfort. List them anyway. The fact that they came to mind suggests they may need resolution. As you list them, give each specific event a title, like it's a short movie, such as: Mom slapped me that time in the car; I stole my brother's baseball cap; I slipped and fell

in front of everybody at the ice skating rink; My third-grade class ridiculed me when I gave that speech; Dad locked me in the toolshed overnight; Mrs. Simmons told me I was dumb.

2. When your list is finished, choose the biggest dominoes on your board, that is, the events that have the most emotional charge for you. Apply EFT to them, one at a time, until the SUD level for each event is 0. You might find yourself laughing about an event that used to bring you to tears; you might find a memory fading. Pay attention to any aspects that arise and treat them as separate dominoes, by tapping for each aspect separately. Make sure you tap on each event until it is resolved. If you find yourself unable to rate the intensity of a bad event on the 0-to-10 scale, you might be dissociating, or repressing a memory. One solution to this problem is to tap 10 rounds of EFT on every aspect of the event you are able to recall. You might then find the event emerging into clearer focus but without the same high degree of emotional charge.

3. After you have removed the biggest dominoes, pick the next biggest, and work on down the line.

4. If you can, clear at least one of your specific events, preferably three, daily for 3 months. By taking only minutes per day, in 3 months you will have cleared 90 to 270 specific events. You will likely discover that your body feels better, that your threshold for getting upset is much lower,

your relationships have improved, and many of your old issues have disappeared. If you revisit specific events you wrote down in your Personal Peace Procedure journal, you will likely discover that their former intensity has evaporated. Pay attention to improvements in your blood pressure, pulse, and respiratory capacity. EFT often produces subtle but measurable changes in your health, and you may miss them if you aren't looking for them.

5. After knocking down all your dominoes, you may feel so much better that you're tempted to alter the dosages of medications your doctor has prescribed. Never make any such changes without consulting your physician. Your doctor is your partner in your healing journey. Tell your doctor that you're working on your emotional issues with EFT, as most health care professionals are acutely aware of the contribution that stress makes to disease.

The Personal Peace Procedure does not take the place of EFT training, nor does it take the place of assistance from a qualified EFT practitioner. It is an excellent supplement to EFT workshops and help from EFT practitioners. EFT's resources are designed to work in combination for the most effective healing results.

Is It Working Yet?

Sometimes EFT's benefits are blindingly obvious. In the introductory video on the home page of the EFT

Universe website, you see a TV reporter with a lifelong fear of spiders receiving a tapping session. Afterward, in a dramatic turnaround, she's able to stroke a giant hairy tarantula spider she's holding in the palm of her hand.

Other times, EFT's effects are subtler and you have to pay close attention to spot them. A friend of mine who has had a lifelong fear of driving in high-speed traffic remarked to me recently that her old fear is completely gone. Over the past year, each time she felt anxious about driving, she pulled her car to the side of the road and tapped. It took many trips and much tapping, but subtle changes gradually took effect. Thanks to EFT, she has emotional freedom and drives without fear. She also has another great benefit, in the form of a closer bond with her daughter and baby granddaughter. They live a 2-hour drive away and, previously, her dread of traffic kept her from visiting them. Now she's able to make the drive with joyful anticipation of playing with her granddaughter.

If you seem not to be making progress on a particular problem despite using EFT, look for other positive changes that might be happening in your life. Stress affects every system in the body, and once you relieve it with EFT, you might find improvements in unexpected areas. For instance, when stressed, the capillaries in your digestive system constrict, impeding digestion. Many people with digestive problems report improvement after EFT. Stress also redistributes biological resources away from your reproductive system. You'll find many stories on EFT Universe of people whose sex lives improved dramatically as a by-product of healing emotional issues.

Stress affects your muscular and circulatory systems; many people report that muscle aches and pains disappear after EFT, and their blood circulation improves. Just as stress is pervasive, relaxation is pervasive, and when with EFT we release our emotional bonds, the relaxing effects are felt all over the body. So perhaps your sore knee has only improved slightly, but you're sleeping better, having fewer respiratory problems, and getting along better with your coworkers.

Saying the Right Words

A common misconception is that you have to say just the right words while tapping in order for EFT to be effective. The truth is that focusing on the problem is more important than the exact words you're using. It's the exposure to the troubling issue that directs healing energy to the right place; the words are just a guide.

Many practitioners write down tapping scripts with lists of affirmations you can use. These can be useful. However, your own words are usually able to capture the full intensity of your emotions in a way that is not possible using other people's words. The way you form language is associated with the configuration of the neural network in your brain. You want the neural pathways along which stress signals travel to be very active while you tap. Using your own wording is more likely to awaken that neural pathway fully than using even the most eloquent wording suggested by someone else. By all means, use tapping scripts if they're available, to nudge you in the right direction. At the same time, utilize the power of prolonged exposure by focusing your mind completely on your own experience. Your mind and body have a healing wisdom that usually directs healing power toward the place where it is most urgently required.

The Next Steps on Your EFT Journey

Now that you've entered the world of EFT, you'll find it to be a rich and supportive place. On the EFT Universe website, you'll find stories written by thousands of people, from all over the world, describing success with an enormous variety of problems. Locate success stories on your particular problem by using the site's drop-down menu, which lists issues alphabetically: Addictions, ADHD, Anxiety, Depression, and so on. Read these stories for insights on how to apply EFT to your particular case. They'll inspire you in your quest for full healing.

Our certified practitioners are a wonderful resource. They've gone through rigorous training in Clinical EFT and have honed their skills with many clients. Many of them work via telephone or videoconferencing, so if you don't find the perfect practitioner in your geographic area, you can still get expert help with remote sessions. Though EFT is primarily a self-help tool and you can get great results alone, you'll find the insight that comes from an outside observer can often alert you to behavior patterns and solutions you can't find by yourself.

Take an EFT workshop. EFT Universe offers more than a 100 workshops each year, all over the world, and you're likely to find Level 1 and 2 workshops close to you.

You'll make friends, see expert demonstrations, and learn EFT systematically. Each workshop contains eight learning modules, and each module builds on the one before. Fifteen years' experience in training thousands of people in EFT has shown us exactly how people learn EFT competently and quickly, and provided the background knowledge to design these trainings. Read the many testimonials on the website to see how deeply transformational the EFT workshops are.

The EFT Universe newsletter is the medium that keeps the whole EFT world connected. Read the stories published there weekly to stay inspired and to learn about new uses for EFT. Write your own experiences and submit them to the newsletter. Post comments on the EFT Universe Facebook page, and comment on the blogs.

If you'd like to help others access the benefits you have gained from EFT, you might consider volunteering your services. There are dozens of ways to support EFT's growth and progress. You can join a tapping circle, or start one yourself. You can donate to EFT research and humanitarian efforts. You can offer tapping sessions to suffering people through one of EFT's humanitarian projects, like those that have reached thousands in Haiti, Rwanda, and elsewhere. You can let your friends know about EFT.

EFT has reached millions of people worldwide with its healing magic but is still in its infancy. By reading this book and practicing this work, you're joining a healing revolution that has the potential to radically reduce human suffering. Imagine if the benefits you've already experienced could be shared by every child, every sick person, every anxious or stressed person in the world. The trajectory of human history would be very different. I'm committed to helping create this shift however I can, and I invite you to join me and all the other people of goodwill in making this vision of a transformed future a reality.

Options and Variations

The Basic Recipe you just learned, with its seven points plus the Karate Chop point, is all you need to get started with EFT. In this chapter, you will learn some additional points that can be helpful for you to know and use.

The first set of these points combined with the points of the Basic Recipe make up what is known as the Full Basic Recipe (see the appendix).

These points are:

- BN = Below the Nipple
- Th = Thumb
- IF = Index Finger
- MF = Middle Finger
- BF = Baby Finger

Additional Points for the Full Basic Recipe

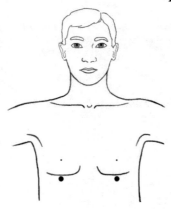

Below the Nipple (BN) points.

Below the Nipple: For men, 1 inch below the nipple. For women, where the underskin of the breast meets the chest wall. This point is abbreviated **BN** for Below the Nipple.

Thumb (Th) point.

Thumb: On the outside edge of your thumb at a point even with the base of the thumbnail. This point is abbreviated **Th** for Thumb.

Index Finger (IF) point.

Index Finger: On the side of your index finger (the side facing your thumb) at a point even with the base of the fingernail. This point is abbreviated **IF** for Index Finger.

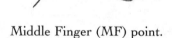

Middle Finger (MF) point.

Middle Finger: On the side of your middle finger (the side closest to your thumb) at a point even with the base of the fingernail. This point is abbreviated **MF** for Middle Finger.

Baby Finger (BF) point.

Baby Finger: On the inside of your baby finger (the side closest to your thumb) at a point even with the base of the fingernail. This point is abbreviated **BF** for Baby Finger.

The abbreviations for these points, combined with the seven from the Basic Recipe plus the Karate Chop point, in the order in which they are tapped, are as follows:

EB = Beginning of the EyeBrow

SE = Side of the Eye

UE = Under the Eye

UN = Under the Nose

Ch = Chin

CB = Beginning of the CollarBone

UA = Under the Arm

BN = Below the Nipple

Th = Thumb

IF = Index Finger

MF = Middle Finger

BF = Baby Finger

KC = Karate Chop

Please notice that these tapping points proceed *down the body*. That is, each tapping point is *below* the one before it. That makes it easy to memorize. After a few rounds, you will likely find yourself tapping through the points without needing to concentrate on the locations.

Note that the ring finger is not included in this list because it is considered redundant or unnecessary. Many EFT practitioners include it for convenience, however.

The **BN** point is also often left out of the sequence because it is awkward for women to tap on that point when in a public setting. Even though EFT works well without it, I include it here for completeness. That way, you have all the points at your command and can choose to try them out. People often discover that they are drawn to tapping on certain points, and when they include these points in their tapping rounds, the results tend to be better. You might want to experiment with all the points to see if this is true for you.

The 9 Gamut Point and Procedure

The 9 Gamut Procedure is, perhaps, the oddest looking process in EFT. Its purpose is to fine-tune the brain and it does so via eye movements, humming, and counting. Through connecting nerves, movement of the eyes stimulates certain regions of the brain. Similarly, the right side of the brain (the creative side) is engaged when you hum a song and the left side (the digital side) is engaged when you count.

The 9 Gamut Procedure is a 10-second process in which nine brain-stimulating actions are performed while continuously tapping on one of the body's energy points, the Gamut point. It has been found, after years of experience, that this routine can add efficiency to EFT and hasten your progress toward emotional freedom, especially when inserted between two rounds of the Sequence.

One way to help memorize the Full Basic Recipe is to look at it as a sandwich. The Setup is the preparation for making the sandwich and the sandwich itself consists of two slices of bread (the Sequence) with the filling, or middle portion, as the 9 Gamut Procedure.

Gamut point.

To do the 9 Gamut Procedure, you must first locate the Gamut point. It is on the back of either hand and is half an inch behind the midpoint between the knuckles at the base of the ring finger and the little finger.

If you draw an imaginary line between the knuckles at the base of the ring finger and little finger and consider that line to be the base of an equilateral triangle whose other sides converge to a point (apex) in the direction of the wrist, then the Gamut point would be located at the apex of the triangle.

Next, you must perform nine different actions while tapping the Gamut point continuously. These nine Gamut actions are:

1. Close your eyes.
2. Open your eyes.
3. Look down hard right while holding your head steady.
4. Look down hard left while holding your head steady.

5. Roll your eyes in a circle as though your nose is at the center of a clock and you are trying to see all the numbers in order. Hold your head steady.

6. Roll your eyes in a circle in the reverse direction. Hold your head steady.

7. Hum 2 seconds of a song (e.g., "Happy Birthday" or "Twinkle, Twinkle, Little Star).

8. Count rapidly from 1 to 5.

9. Hum 2 seconds of a song again.

Note that these nine actions are presented in a certain order and I suggest that you memorize them in the order given. You can mix the order up if you wish, however, so long as you do all nine of them *and* you perform the last three together as a unit. That is, you hum for 2 seconds, then count, then hum the song again, in that order. Years of experience have proven this to be important.

Note that, for some people, humming "Happy Birthday" causes resistance because it brings up memories of unhappy birthdays. In that case, you can either use EFT on those unhappy memories and resolve them, or you can sidestep this issue for now by substituting some other song.

Many EFT practitioners routinely use the 9 Gamut Procedure in cases of trauma. The following account by Tana Clark explains why she thinks it has made all the difference for her daughter.

Excessive Emotionality in a Brain-Damaged Child

by Tana Clark

I am an EFT practitioner and have a daughter who is brain damaged from birth. She did not get enough oxygen due to the cord around her neck for a lengthy time. I work with her almost on a daily basis with EFT. She can become very emotional at times, and it seems to take her hours to get over it. I have tapped with her on many occasions for this problem. I noticed that if I did not do the Gamut point, she didn't seem to settle down.

Finally, I just started doing the Gamut point when she "got stuck in the right brain." Now when she gets stuck, we immediately do a sequence and the 9 Gamut Procedure, and have 100% success rate to evaporate her emotion. When people get extremely emotional and can't seem to find a way out, they are stuck in the right brain.

Many people have problems being stuck in the right brain, and many of us have had the experience where we just can't stop crying. Doing the eye movements keeps our brain moving from right brain to left brain to right brain. It helps the brain to work together instead of being stuck on one side.

I also used it for a teenager whose family was moving; she was very upset about it and kept crying and crying. No amount of the other parts of EFT helped her feel less emotional. We moved to the 9 Gamut Procedure and, like magic, the tears dried up.

Using the short form of EFT, we often leave out the 9 Gamut Procedure. But if there is a large amount of emotion, it is extremely helpful. I couldn't do without it.

❊ ❊ ❊

The Sore Spot

The Sore Spot is another point often used in EFT. There are two Sore Spots and it doesn't matter which one you use. They are located in the upper left and right portions of the chest and you find them as follows:

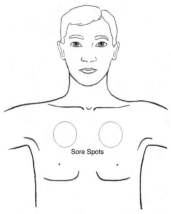

The Sore Spot.

Go to the base of the throat about where a man would knot his tie. Poke around in this area and you will find a U-shaped notch at the top of your sternum (breastbone). From the top of that notch, go down 2 or 3 inches toward your navel and then move over 2 or 3 inches to your left (or right). You should now be in the upper left (or right) portion of your chest. If you press vigorously in that area (within a 2-inch radius) you will find a "Sore Spot." This is the place you will need to rub while saying the Setup.

This spot is usually sore or tender when you rub it vigorously because lymphatic congestion occurs there. When you rub it, you are dispersing that congestion.

Fortunately, after a few rounds, the congestion is all dispersed and the soreness goes away. Then you can rub it with no discomfort whatsoever.

I don't mean to overplay the soreness you may feel. It's not like you will have massive, intense pain by rubbing this Sore Spot. It is certainly bearable and should cause no undue discomfort. If it does, then lighten your pressure a little.

Also, if you've had some kind of operation in that area of the chest or if there is any medical reason whatsoever why you shouldn't be probing around in that specific area, then switch to the other side. Both sides are equally effective. In any case, if there is any doubt, consult your health practitioner before proceeding. Or tap the Karate Chop point instead.

A Few Optional Points

As EFT spread to those with a knowledge of acupuncture, many students and practitioners began to add tapping points. There are hundreds of acupuncture points on the human body—in fact, it's just about impossible to tap on yourself anywhere without hitting one or more of them—but the most popular optional points in EFT circles are probably the top of the head and points on the wrists and ankles. Feel free to experiment with them to see if they are helpful for you.

Top of Head. Run an imaginary string over your head from the top of one ear to the top of the other. The highest point that the string reaches is the Top of Head point. It is set slightly back from the center of the top of your head.

Wrists. Several meridians run through the inside and outside of the wrist. An easy way to stimulate all of the wrist points is to cross your wrists and tap them together (about where your wristwatch would be), inside wrist against inside wrist, inside wrist against outside wrist, and outside wrist against outside wrist. You can also slap lightly on the wrist with the flat of the opposite hand.

Ankles. Several meridians run through the ankles. The points here are less widely used because they're less convenient. To stimulate these points, simply tap on all sides of either or both ankles.

In the reports shared by EFT users in this book and on the EFT website, other points are mentioned, including some that are used in combination. As I don't personally use these points or combinations, I won't elaborate on them here.

Putting It All Together

Now that you have learned the ingredients of the Full Basic Recipe, here is how a complete EFT treatment works using it. For this example, we'll focus on a physical symptom—a headache—but we use the same basic procedure to address other aspects of posttraumatic stress disorder. Most people with PTSD feel anxious when they encounter EFT for the first time, and their anxiety produces physical symptoms such as headaches, a feeling of tightness in the stomach, nausea, dizziness, tense shoulder muscles, or an inability to take a deep, relaxed breath. Any of these symptoms can be an excellent "first problem" to treat with EFT.

What is the problem? I have a headache.

How bad is it? It's pretty serious. On a scale from 1 to 10, it's an 8.

Setup: Tap the Karate Chop point or rub the Sore Spot while saying:

> *Even though I have this headache, I fully and completely accept myself.*

> *Even though I have this headache, I fully and completely accept myself.*

> *Even though I have this headache, I fully and completely accept myself.*

The Sequence: Tap each point while repeating your Reminder Phrase.

EB = Beginning of the EyeBrow: *This headache*

SE = Side of the Eye: *This headache*

UE = Under the Eye: *This headache*

UN = Under the Nose: *This headache*

Ch = Chin: *This headache*

CB = Beginning of the CollarBone: *This headache*

UA = Under the Arm: *This headache*

BN = Below the Nipple: *This headache*

Th = Thumb: *This headache*

IF = Index Finger: *This headache*

MF = Middle Finger: *This headache*

BF = **B**aby **F**inger: *This headache*

KC = **K**arate **C**hop: *This headache*

9 Gamut Procedure: Tap the Gamut point while doing the following:

1. Close your eyes.

2. Open your eyes.

3. Eyes hard down right while holding the head steady.

4. Eyes hard down left while holding the head steady.

5. Roll your eyes around in a circle in one direction.

6. Roll your eyes in a circle in the reverse direction.

7. Hum 2 seconds of a song.

8. Count rapidly from 1 to 5.

9. Hum 2 seconds of a song again.

Repeat the Sequence: Tap each point while repeating your Reminder Phrase.

EB = Beginning of the **E**ye**B**row: *This headache*

SE = **S**ide of the **E**ye: *This headache*

UE = **U**nder the **E**ye: *This headache*

UN = **U**nder the **N**ose: *This headache*

Ch = **Ch**in: *This headache*

CB = Beginning of the **C**ollar**B**one: *This headache*

UA = **U**nder the **A**rm: *This headache*

BN = **B**elow the **N**ipple: *This headache*

Th = **Th**umb: *This headache*

IF = **I**ndex **F**inger: *This headache*

MF = Middle Finger: *This headache*

BF = Baby Finger: *This headache*

KC = Karate Chop: *This headache*

You have now finished a complete round of EFT's Full Basic Recipe. The next thing to do is evaluate your progress.

How does it feel now? If the headache has completely disappeared, congratulations, you're done. No further treatment is needed. For the purposes of this example, we'll say that the pain has gone down to a 3 or 4. It doesn't hurt as much as it did, but it's still there.

Adjusted Setup: Tap the Karate Chop point or rub the Sore Spot while saying:

> *Even though I still have some of this headache, I fully and completely accept myself.*

> *Even though I still have some of this headache, I fully and completely accept myself.*

> *Even though I still have some of this headache, I fully and completely accept myself.*

The Sequence: Tap each point while repeating your Reminder Phrase.

EB: *Remaining headache*

SE: *Remaining headache*

UE: *Remaining headache*

UN: *Remaining headache*

Ch: *Remaining headache*

CB: *Remaining headache*

UA: *Remaining headache*

BN: *Remaining headache*

Th: *Remaining headache*

IF: *Remaining headache*

MF: *Remaining headache*

BF: *Remaining headache*

KC: *Remaining headache*

9 Gamut Procedure: Tap the Gamut point while doing the following:

1. Close your eyes.

2. Open your eyes.

3. Eyes hard down right while holding the head steady.

4. Eyes hard down left while holding the head steady.

5. Roll your eyes around in a circle in one direction.

6. Roll your eyes in a circle in the reverse direction.

7. Hum 2 seconds of a song.

8. Count rapidly from 1 to 5.

9. Hum 2 seconds of a song again.

The Sequence: Tap each point while repeating your Reminder Phrase.

EB: *Remaining headache*

SE: *Remaining headache*

UE: *Remaining headache*

UN: *Remaining headache*

Ch: *Remaining headache*

CB: *Remaining headache*

UA: *Remaining headache*

BN: *Remaining headache*

Th: *Remaining headache*

IF: *Remaining headache*

MF: *Remaining headache*

BF: *Remaining headache*

KC: *Remaining headache*

You have now completed an entire EFT treatment for headache pain. You will use the same procedure to apply EFT's Full Basic Recipe to any problem.

More About the Acceptance Phrase

The first element of every EFT Setup is a statement about the problem. The second part, the acceptance phrase, is just as important. The combined statement says that, even though I have this problem, I accept myself. The acceptance phrase is an affirmation, which I consider crucial to the effectiveness of EFT.

For many who try EFT, however, the Setup is a stumbling block. In a typical workshop of several hundred people, as many as half feel uncomfortable saying, "I fully and completely accept myself." For some, the incongruity is so severe that they can't say it at all.

EFT can help anyone resolve old emotional issues that contribute to low self-esteem or feelings of guilt or shame, but for now, if the Setup is a problem for you or your client, try saying one of the following statements while you tap:

> *Even though I can't yet fully and completely accept myself, I would like someday to fully and completely accept myself.*

> *Even though I can't quite fully and completely accept myself, I'll be okay.*

> *Even though it's hard for me to say that I fully and completely accept myself, I can let go of that for now and do this work.*

> *Even though I don't yet accept myself, I can and do acknowledge myself.*

If the acceptance phrase causes intense emotional pain or discomfort, or if it feels totally untrue, try changing the Setup altogether to something like:

> *Even though I have this _____, I would like to feel better.*

> *Even though I have this feeling of sadness, I can enjoy life.*

> *Even though I have this tightness in my stomach, I can relax.*

> *Even though I have this anger and frustration, it's going away.*

> *Even though I'm worried and don't know what to expect, I choose peace.*

As you experiment with Setups, try different variations. For example, try saying,

Even though I feel _____, I absolutely do accept myself.

Even though I feel very upset, I would like to love and forgive myself.

Even though I feel guilty about what happened, I forgive myself and anyone and anything that contributed in any way to this feeling.

Setups, by the way, can be of any length. While tapping on the Karate Chop point or massaging the Sore Spot, say whatever you like about the problem. You can also talk *to* the problem. The more detailed, specific, colorful, and interesting your Setup, the more likely you are to experience good results. As you read examples throughout this book of how people have worked with EFT, you'll begin to appreciate the important role that imagination and intuition play in this process. Be ready to let your own imagination and intuition work on your behalf as you start tapping.

In the following article, EFT practitioner Betty Moore-Hafter shares her recommendations for softening the delivery of EFT's acceptance phrase. Her approach is ideal for those who need to tiptoe into their issues, which includes a good percentage of the PTSD population. Try any of these acceptance phrases on yourself and on others, and experiment with your own variations. Beginning with the right Setup is part of the "art of delivery," saving considerable time and discomfort in EFT sessions dealing with complex problems.

Soft Language to
Ease the EFT Acceptance Phrase

by Betty Moore-Hafter

As I understand it, the EFT Setup paves the way for healing by shifting the hard, locked-up energy of Psychological Reversal to the softer energy of self-acceptance. I have found that creative wording can be especially helpful toward this end. Here are some of my favorites:

1. "With kindness and compassion" or "without judgment."

These and similar words contribute an extra dimension of support and care, especially when the issue is a sensitive one. Tears often come to people's eyes as we add these simple words.

> *Even though I feel unworthy, I deeply and completely accept myself with kindness and compassion—it's been hard for me.*

> *Even though I'm so afraid of rejection, I deeply accept myself with gentleness and compassion—I've been hurt a lot.*

> *Even though I feel guilty for that mistake I made, I totally accept myself without judgment. I'm only human.*

2. "I want to bring healing to this."

Some people balk at the words "I deeply accept myself" and say, "But I don't accept myself! I hate myself for this." One gentle way to proceed is to say:

> *Even though I don't accept myself, I can accept that this is just where I am right now. And even though I*

don't accept myself, I want to bring healing to this. I would like to feel better, find more peace, and reach more self-acceptance.

3. "The truth is..."

These words can usher in powerful reframes. And when you reframe a situation while tapping, it does shift the energy and things begin to change.

Even though I crave this cigarette, the truth is, cigarettes are making me sick.

Even though I still feel guilty, the truth is, I've done nothing wrong. This is false guilt.

Even though I still feel responsible for my sister, the truth is, she is an adult. She's responsible for herself now.

4. "I'm willing to see it differently."

Sometimes amazing things happen after adding the words "I'm willing to see it differently." One of my clients was convinced that she could never have a child because she might abandon that child the way her father abandoned her. As we tapped through her pain from the father issue, I began adding the phrase, "and I'm willing to see it differently."

Even though my father really hurt me, I love and accept myself, and I'm willing to see it differently.

After several rounds of tapping, she seemed calm and said thoughtfully, "You know, I think my father really did love me in his own way. That's all he was capable of." She felt at peace with it for the first time. And, when I heard from her later, she and her husband were talking about having children. She knew she was not her father and would do it differently. She saw it all differently.

5. "That was then and this is now."

When childhood pain is being healed, people often feel great relief when words like the following are added.

> *Even though when I was 8 years old, I cried alone and no one came, I deeply love and accept my young self. And that was then and this is now. Now I have lots of help and support.*

> *Even though I still feel anxious, afraid that something bad will happen, I deeply accept myself. And even though my child self felt anxious all the time, afraid my father would explode, I love and accept that child self. That was then and this is now. Now I'm safe. I don't need this hypervigilance anymore. I can relax now.*

6. "I'm open to the possibility…"

"Choice" statements are, of course, very empowering when we are ready for them. But sometimes stating a choice is too much of a stretch. Often, the gentlest way to introduce a better choice is simply to bring in the idea of possibility.

> *Even though I'm full of doubt that I can lose weight, I deeply accept myself and I'm open to the possibility that it may be easier than I think.*

> *Even though I'm stuck in this anger and don't want to let it go, I'm open to the possibility that it would be nice to feel more peaceful about this.*

Even though I don't think EFT will work for me, I deeply accept myself and I'm willing to entertain the possibility that maybe EFT will help. I'm ready for some help.

I believe that when we open the door of possibility just a crack, it is enough to set the healing process in motion.

With all of these phrases, you can keep "I deeply and completely accept myself" and add the extra phrase, or you can substitute the phrase. Experiment and see what works for you!

* * *

And there are more variations. Instead of saying, "I completely and fully accept myself," you can simply say:

I'm okay.	*I'll be okay.*
I'll feel better soon.	*Everything's improving.*

Or something similar. This, by the way, is how we use EFT with children. The phrase "I fully and completely accept myself" makes little sense to kids. Instead, a child who is upset can say something like the following:

Even though I flunked the math test, I'm a cool kid, I'm okay.

Even though I lost my backpack and I'm mad at myself, I'm still an awesome kid.

More Notes on Positive Setups

In addition to adding acceptance phrases that help the user feel relaxed and confident, you can improve the effectiveness of Setups by adding a phrase or two that reinforces positive results.

EFT practitioner Angela Treat Lyon says, "I also use the phrase *'because I love and accept myself,'* which I start as soon as it's apparent that the person has shifted to making new choices. This is very empowering. And lately I've been using *'because I love and believe in myself,'* which is also really powerful."

Dr. Phillip Mountrose and Dr. Jane Mountrose use what they call a "Miracle Reframe," in which they add to the Setup the phrase "Anything is possible and miracles are happening now":

Even though I have this _____, I know that anything is possible and miracles are happening now.

As they explain, improvements occur rapidly when we align ourselves with "higher vibrations."

Another way to make setups more positive is to use Dr. Patricia Carrington's Choices Method, which she explains in chapter 8.

With EFT, you can tap a problem out, and with the same basic technique, you can tap a solution in. Nothing is more versatile than that! No matter how you phrase your Setup, tapping on your EFT points will help, but tapping on both "problem" and "solution" phrases will help bring about long-lasting positive changes in record time.

The Apex Effect

As you practice EFT and show others how to use it, you'll hear all kinds of explanations as to how or why it works.

We use the term Apex Effect, which was coined by Dr. Roger Callahan, to describe these explanations. They all indicate clients' propensity to explain away their obvious relief. To some people, it is just not believable that tapping could produce these results, so they attempt to explain the improvements by other means. Clients say that the problem went away because they "can't think about it anymore." Upon investigation, however, it is discovered that they can, indeed, recount the formerly traumatic incident in great detail. What they really mean is that they can't think about the problem *in the same way* as before.

Sometimes they say, "All that tapping confused me" or "The tapping is a distraction." Or clients will say, "All those years of previous therapy finally worked for me." They achieve relief immediately after or during tapping, but, to them, tapping couldn't have been the true cause of their new freedom. Why? Because it doesn't "compute" or match their belief systems. Their minds cannot make sense of it. So they conclude that the results must have come from "real" therapy (talk therapy, etc.) and somehow, as if by magic, all that previous emotional work chose this moment to become effective. This is nonsensical, of course, but some people are more comfortable believing such explanations than giving credit to tapping, which their minds cannot explain.

In some cases, the client honestly doesn't remember how distressed, uncomfortable, anxious, stressed, or in pain he or she was at the beginning of an EFT session. Keeping track of the person's "before" picture, complete with its rating on the intensity scale, serves as documentation of changes that occur with tapping.

In the end, though, it doesn't matter who or what gets the credit. What matters is that the person feels better. That's what EFT is all about.

One thing I can say with confidence is that it is just about impossible to do EFT incorrectly. People have gotten good results when tapping on "wrong" EFT points, by omitting or forgetting some points, by tapping on a single point rather than the entire Sequence, by tapping on the points in reverse order, or by tapping mentally, without touching the points. They have changed the Setup so it bears little resemblance to the Setup you learned here. And EFT still worked. I will remind you again that the Basic Recipe is simply a starting place and that, once you understand it, you can experiment with EFT variations, including the ones covered in this chapter.

Borrowing Benefits

One of the most profound discoveries in EFT in the early part of the 21st century was the phenomenon called "Borrowing Benefits." It's the discovery that simply watching someone else do EFT on their issues, while tapping along with them, can help reduce the emotional intensity of your own issues.

Borrowing Benefits was first noted by EFT practitioners. They reported that, rather than feeling exhausted after a day working with clients, they were energized. Their own emotional problems seemed to have melted away, even though they weren't working on the same issues as their clients.

This might seem hard to believe at first, because it doesn't apply to most other methods. Talk therapists don't usually find their own anxiety or depression improving after working with clients. Social workers don't find their problems melting after a day of work. The reverse often occurs, as they take on the emotional burdens their clients are processing. The rate of burnout in the helping professions is high.

You don't get the benefits of meditation by watching other people meditate. The problems of life coaches aren't necessarily resolved when they help their clients resolve their own problems with motivation, accountability, or goal setting.

Yet just watching EFT sessions and tapping along on your issues can produce lasting change.

The first study to examine this phenomenon was performed by Jack Rowe, PhD, then a professor at Texas A&M University. He examined the mental health of 108 people attending an EFT weekend workshop. He tested them a month before the workshop, and immediately before, and found that their levels were unchanged. But after the workshop, they had improved dramatically, even though they were watching sessions performed onstage.

They retained a part of the improvement when Dr. Rowe tested them at subsequent intervals (Rowe, 2005).

The Rowe study was replicated and extended in a second study by a research team that included me and Audrey Brooks, PhD, a professor at the psychology department of the University of Arizona at Tucson (Church & Brooks, 2010). We looked at mental health symptoms in 218 healthcare professionals such as doctors, nurses, psychotherapists, chiropractors, and alternative medicine practitioners. The subjects were attendees at five professional conferences who attended a 1-day EFT workshop. At one of the conferences, EFT was offered by one EFT expert, and at the other four by me.

Participant mental health improved significantly at all five conferences. As we measured their symptoms during a follow-up period, we discovered that they retained most of their gains. We also tracked whether or not participants used EFT after the workshop, and found that those who did more EFT got better than those who did less EFT.

A later replication of the study examined workshops taught by EFT Masters, such as Ann Adams, Loretta Sparks, and Carol Look. It reinforced the same findings, and showed that EFT is effective regardless of which EFT expert offers the workshop (Palmer-Hoffman & Brooks, 2011).

This makes three studies measuring the effects of EFT on hundreds of people, and provides compelling evidence for the effectiveness of Borrowing Benefits.

You can receive the emotional advantages of Borrowing Benefits by attending an EFT workshop. You can also use the videos on the EFT Universe website. We've recorded a number of sessions that you can simply tap along with. Go to the video page, choose a session, and tap along.

Here are the instructions for Borrowing Benefits:

1. **Pick an issue you'd like to work on**. Write down a brief name for the issue in 1 to 3 words.

2. **Rate your degree of emotional distress on a scale from 0 to 10**, with 0 being no intensity and 10 being the maximum intensity. Write down your number.

3. **Identify a part of your body in which you feel the sensation associated with that number**, and write down the name of that particular body location.

4. **Recall an event in your life when you felt that feeling in your body**. Pick the event that occurred the earliest in your life, if possible.

5. **Start tapping through the EFT points**, as soon as the video session starts, and keep tapping till the end. When the person onscreen states their issue, state your issue instead.

6. **When the video is done**, usually in 5 to 20 minutes, think about the issue, tune in to that same part of your body, and rate your degree of emotional distress a second time. Write down your new number.

You'll usually find that your number dropped substantially. If it didn't, then pick another specific incident in your life most identified with that feeling in your body, and repeat the process.

Tapping for PTSD

To apply EFT's Basic Recipe to posttraumatic stress disorder, you can begin with any physical symptom or anything the person wants to focus on, but an excellent way to start is with a general statement that does not involve a specific memory or event.

Those who have already studied EFT know that this goes against the advice to begin with specific events rather than vague or general statements. However, treating trauma cases can be very different from using EFT to help someone lose weight, fix a sore back, or improve a golf game. Because the events that trigger PTSD can be so intense, tiptoeing up on them, approaching them gently and gradually, and starting with vague, general, or "global" statements can be an excellent idea. This has the advantage of "taking the edge off" the problem so that deeper work can be done with much less emotional pain

If you are an experienced practitioner already familiar with PTSD, starting with a specific intrusive memory can be the fastest way to clear both the memory and all of the problems associated with it, but this may cause acute discomfort and an increase in PTSD symptoms. Throughout this book, you will find examples of both approaches. I present the "general description" Setup first because I consider it relatively safe as well as effective, and I encourage anyone who is new to EFT or to working with PTSD to try it first.

Example of the Basic Recipe Applied to a General Description

The following sample Setup Statements introduce EFT gently by working around a problem rather than confronting it directly. Note that it does not describe what happened. This type of Setup is recommended for anyone who does not feel ready to focus on a traumatic event, who seems overcome with emotion, or who is highly skeptical and does not yet feel a sense of rapport with his or her practitioner or instructor.

Try starting with one of these Setup Statements, or create something similar. The following examples all end with "I fully and completely accept myself."

Setup (tap the KC point or massage the Sore Spot):

Even though I feel overwhelmed, I fully and completely accept myself.

Even though I don't expect this tapping business to help me at all...

Even though I don't want to think about what went on over there...

Even though I'm afraid to try something new...

Even though I've already tried everything and have been disappointed...

Even though I feel discouraged...

Even though nothing has helped me get my old life back...

Say the Setup Statement three times.

The Sequence (tap the EFT points from head to hands):

While tapping the EFT points in sequence, say an appropriate Reminder Phrase, such as:

Don't want to think... Don't want to think... Don't want to think...

Overwhelmed... Overwhelmed... Overwhelmed...

Nothing helps... Nothing helps... Nothing helps...

9 Gamut Procedure: While tapping the Gamut point, close your eyes, open your eyes, look down hard right, look down hard left, roll your eyes in one direction, roll them in the opposite direction, hum a few bars of a tune, count from 1 to 5, and hum again.

Repeat the Sequence, saying the Reminder Phrase. Often after a full round of tapping for a general Setup, the person feels calmer and more comfortable.

At this point, you can repeat the entire round of EFT tapping for the same general Setup or you can switch topics or use a different Setup for the same general theme.

By starting with a general theme or a nonspecific statement, you introduce EFT gently, giving the person time to get used to the procedure and experience its results before going on to more serious issues.

If you suffer from PTSD yourself, general statements are an excellent way to begin because they build a foundation so that when you do address specific memories, you'll be more prepared, you'll feel more comfortable, and your results will be more effective. For more detailed do-it-yourself instructions, see chapter 11.

Example of the Basic Recipe Applied to a Specific Memory

In this next example, the person is haunted by a powerful explosion and feels ready to talk about it. We start by asking the person to measure his or her discomfort on a scale from 0 to 10.

Measure intensity. Rate the discomfort level from 0 to 10 on the intensity scale.

Setup (tap the KC point or massage the Sore Spot):

Even though I have this recurring flashback to the moment of the explosion, I fully and completely accept myself.

Even though I have this recurring flashback to the moment of the explosion, I fully and completely accept myself.

Even though I have this recurring flashback to the moment of the explosion, I fully and completely accept myself.

The Sequence (EFT points from head to hands):

Explosion…Explosion…Explosion…Explosion…

9 Gamut Procedure: While tapping the Gamut point, close your eyes, open your eyes, look down hard right, look down hard left, roll your eyes in one direction, roll them in the opposite direction, hum a tune, count from 1 to 5, and hum a tune.

Repeat the Sequence:

Explosion…Explosion…Explosion…Explosion…

Measure intensity. If the level has gone down to 0, the person will be able to remember and talk about this event without being distressed. It no longer triggers emotional intensity.

If the person feels better but is still a little upset or uncomfortable, start over, using this Setup:

Even though I still have some of this recurring flashback to the moment of the explosion, I fully and completely accept myself.

And for the tapping sequence, use the Reminder Phrase:

Remaining recurring explosion…Remaining recurring explosion…Remaining recurring explosion…

As long as the person continues to feel better, this protocol can be repeated several times. When the person feels emotionally neutral (the discomfort level has fallen to 0), this Setup has served its purpose and you can move on.

When thinking about the explosion in a general way no longer generates an emotional response, you can ask the person to describe the event—where it happened, what the person was doing, what day it was, what time it was, what the person saw, heard, smelled, felt, and so on. If any of these questions or recollections make the person uncomfortable, go back a step and start tapping with a new Setup Statement for that specific aspect of the event.

It helps to have the person continue to tap the EFT points while talking. The easiest way to do this is to continue tapping yourself and ask the person to mirror your motions while your conversation continues. This tapping does not involve a Setup Statement or any Reminder Phrases, but it serves an important purpose by releasing energy blocks and maintaining the person's energy balance throughout the conversation.

❋ ❋ ❋

EFT trainer Ann Adams gives us the details, including Setup language, in a relatively simple case involving accident flashbacks. This is a common problem and thus Ann's message is likely to be helpful to many people.

Rapid Relief from Accident Flashbacks

by Ann Adams

Last year, Brenda, one of the terrific cooks at our residential program, had two traffic accidents in less than 6 weeks. The irony was that both accidents occurred at the same intersection on her way home from work.

She didn't break any bones but had whiplash and other physical problems. She had weeks of physical therapy and was out of work for 4 months. She returned to work last August. In November, she shared with me that she was still having flashbacks of the accident and trouble sleeping. Since I was conducting another staff training on using EFT the following week, I suggested she attend.

I started the training session with a brief explanation of the technique and led everyone right into an exercise, explaining that they did not have to believe that this exercise would work. I asked them to pick a specific incident in their life that still upset them when they thought about it and then write down their current intensity on a scale of 0 to 10.

Then we did three group rounds starting with: *"Even though I have this upset feeling, I deeply and completely accept myself."* After two slow deep breaths, I asked them to think about their upset and write down the number again.

The inevitable surprised looks came on some faces. Several said the upset incident didn't bother them anymore. Brenda said, "Oh, my goodness!" and I asked if she'd like to elaborate on that statement. She was working on the second traffic accident and said, "I can still see it happen, but I am calm now. It is over and I am okay." I asked for her number and she said it was a 0. She seemed so comfortable talking about it that I asked if she would like to work on other aspects of the accident as a demonstration in front of the group.

She agreed but wanted to remain seated. I asked her to think of the worst part of the accident and she said she was so afraid of being hit again that she drove 5 extra miles coming and going to work in a detour around the "accident intersection." Her fear of being hit again at that intersection was at least a 9.

We tapped several times for:

Even though I am afraid to drive through the intersection...

Even though I am afraid I will be hit again...

Even though I feel helpless to prevent being hit by a car...

I asked her to picture herself passing that intersection on her way home but to stop at any point she felt herself getting upset again. She began by picturing herself getting in the car, starting it, and then passing each landmark along the way until she got to the intersection where she had had the two wrecks.

She closed her eyes and was quiet for a few seconds. Then she said she was still a little apprehensive when she got close enough to actually see the intersection. Her intensity level was a 6. So we tapped twice through the points for: *"Even though I still have some apprehension about getting close to where the accident happened..."*

When asked to take a deep breath and give me a number, she reported it was now a 2. I told the audience that I wanted to show them another step and for those who still had any level of upset to think about their problem and follow along. So Brenda and the audience did the 9 Gamut Procedure and another round of tapping. Brenda was smiling now and said she thought she could go home the shorter way.

I suggested to Brenda that she use the remaining time in the staff training to work on any other scenes of the accident that still affected her. And, as always, I gave the group a handout that describes the EFT process and encouraged them to use it for everything.

That was in November. About the middle of January, I had an opportunity to ask Brenda about her feelings now about the accident. She said, "That stuff you did really helped." She told me that not only had she been able to drive home the shorter way, but also after the training she was able to sleep and no longer had flashbacks about the cars ramming into her.

But she said that something about it still bothered her—it was a nagging kind of feeling that something was still wrong. Wrong with what? I asked. "Wrong with me," she said. She was meaning emotionally, so I took a guess and said that sometimes victims felt that they were in some way responsible for what had happened to them. She said, "Yes, I feel like I should have been able to do something to stop it. That I shouldn't have been driving by that intersection that day."

We started tapping for:

> *Even though I ought to have been able to do something...*
>
> *Even though I feel responsible...*
>
> *Even though I feel guilty for the accident...*

Brenda then laughed and told me that now she couldn't see how she could have thought she was responsible. There was nothing she could have done to stop it. "It was not my fault."

I asked her to close her eyes again and picture both accidents, including the police and hospital experiences, and to stop at any point there was any upset. About a minute passed and she opened her eyes and said, "That's amazing," commenting on the fact that she had no upset.

* * *

In the next story, which is also about the aftermath of a car accident, Edward Miner tells how he used EFT in a phone session to resolve the physical symptoms and emotions connected to the crash.

Resolution of Vertigo and a Car Crash Memory
by Edward Miner

I am a hypnotherapist and am always looking for better ways to help people get over their problems. Last evening, I talked with my sister, who lives in another state, about a condition of severe vertigo. She was in a minor automobile accident 2 weeks ago, experienced whiplash, and several days later started experiencing the vertigo.

I just got off the phone with her and want to report that she was symptom free when I hung up. In all, it took about 15 minutes to explain EFT and run through it about four times, testing between each run. I initially started the Setup with "Even though I have this vertigo and dizziness, I completely love and accept myself," but didn't see much movement. I adjusted to "Even though I have this vertigo and dizziness, I completely forgive myself or anyone else who may have contributed to it."

After a runthrough and a 9 Gamut Procedure, she was experiencing no symptoms. I had her move around a lot more and she found that when she tipped her head back she still had a dizzy feeling, but the rotation was slower. When I asked her if the feeling had an emotion, she said "annoyance," so we tapped on "the annoyance emotion." Subsequent SUD testing could find no more feelings of dizziness. She was amazed because she said that this was the worst time of day, just before she went to bed, and just prior to taking her medicine.

❈ ❈ ❈

For a bonus chapter entitled:

EFT Choices, Solutions, and Top Ten Tapping Tips

Go to EFTuniverse.com/ptsd-bonus.pdf

The Gentle Techniques

There are many situations in which psychological trauma is overwhelming. EFT's Basic Recipe requires you or your client to focus on a specific event. What do you do when the event is laden with fear, and you don't want to remember it? What about the case of a memory filled with terror and pain, one that you've been pushing from your mind for years or even decades, and cannot bear to think about? How can you apply EFT in such cases? Here are some examples of people who might be unable to do EFT without a gentler or more gradual approach:

- A male veteran in his 70s who committed atrocities against civilians in wartime. His actions occurred long ago and are not known to anyone except him. He's never talked to anyone about what he did, and he is so riddled by guilt that he dissociates, pushing the memories out of his conscious mind. Yet he still has involuntary flashbacks, nightmares, and intrusive thoughts about the people he injured and killed. His SUD score is 10 at the mere thought of talking about these events.

- A 22-year-old woman who, as a child, was ritually abused by her aunt and uncle who raised her. She recently underwent a course of psychotherapy in which memories of the abuse surfaced. She also suffers from unexplained symptoms such as migraine headaches and irregular periods, and has been diagnosed with rheumatoid arthritis.

- A woman, 33, whose husband and children were killed in a car crash. She was the driver and escaped unharmed. Whenever she gets close to thinking about it, she begins to shake and cry uncontrollably.

- A woman in her mid 30s who is disabled by chronic pain. Medical tests are unable to find anything wrong with her, yet her pain is severe in several parts of her body. She has continuous pain in both her shoulders ranging in severity from 4 to 6 on the SUD scale, as well as pain in her right knee that never drops below a 7, and intermittent pain in her left ankle that frequently renders her unable to walk. She's desperate for a cure, yet her case has baffled doctors for years.

- A 55-year-old man who has experienced several losses in the past year. Two weeks ago, his best friend unexpectedly dropped dead of a heart attack while exercising on a treadmill at the gym. The two of them shared the same birthday. His mother died 3 months previously, and his father died 6 months before that after a protracted and agonizing illness.

His wife divorced him just after his father's death, he is estranged from both his children, and he has just lost his job. He has been so buffeted by these losses that he has plunged into a deep depression. His SUD score for general depression is 7 and goes to 10 when he thinks about each particular loss.

- A female therapist who is also an EFT practitioner but who is unable to remember a single event in her childhood before the age of 12. She has tried hard to recover memories but has been unsuccessful, as have several other therapists who have worked with her. She is embarrassed about her "failure." She has an uneasy feeling when she tries to recall earlier events.

- A man is disabled by multiple sclerosis (MS). The disease runs in his family, and genetic testing shows that he has a high susceptibility to it, as well as to pancreatic cancer. The MS has become progressively worse, following a course similar to that of his father.

- A female painter in her 60s who lives in a tiny rented room and has never been able to make any money from her artwork or to save money from any other profession she's tried. Nearing retirement age, she has no savings. She recently had a bout of hepatitis that left her weak and demoralized, and saddled with medical bills that she can't pay. Her family was poor, she was raised in poverty, and her relatives are all, in her words, "financial basket cases." She feels over-whelmed by these problems and despairs of having a better future.

When people have horrific experiences in their past, long-standing family patterns, or overwhelming losses, it's hard to believe that change is possible. Dealing with these issues is very painful, and fraught with the likelihood of failure. Yet in the hands of a skilled practitioner, EFT is able to address these problems and open up the possibility of emotional freedom, even in cases of people suffering deeply.

The Need for Gentle Techniques

One of the most satisfying experiences for any EFT practitioner is to work with people who have carried severe emotional trauma around with them for many years and to witness how quickly it can lift after EFT. Sometimes a client has suffered from a problem for decades and, in a single round of tapping, it is gone. After such a session, a client may appear dazed, as though they'd just awakened from a trance. They may shed many layers of wounding in just a single session. They then move on with their lives, enjoying emotional freedom and no longer carrying around the heavy burden of suffering that had previously weighed them down.

Other times, just a small part of a problem dissolves during an EFT session. A single traumatic event may take multiple sessions to address. Persistent lifetime patterns might take a great deal of persistence as layer after layer of the problem is tapped away over a long period of time. Many of us have traumatic events that are so big and daunting that we hardly know where to begin, and we fear being swept away by the tide of negative emotion associated with them. The Gentle Techniques are useful for addressing psychological wounding that appears overwhelming.

When you work with others in EFT, you will often run into traumatic childhood memories, and you may well have experienced trauma yourself. Unresolved traumatic childhood memories are the foundation of adult maladaptive behaviors and limiting beliefs. More times than not, a person visits an EFT practitioner to address a current issue in their life and it leads them back to earlier pain, loss, and trauma. It becomes apparent that the current life stressor is being made worse by unresolved pain from the past. The previous examples are all drawn from actual cases reported in EFT workshops or recorded in the EFT Universe archives.

You'll find you often need techniques much less confrontive than EFT's basic instruction to "think about the problem." For this reason, EFT uses a suite of methods called the Gentle Techniques, and they're invaluable for these situations. The Gentle Techniques allow a client to tap without having to confront the trauma head on. They gradually reduce the amount of triggering over the course of several rounds of tapping, rendering the triggering event manageable.

There are three Gentle Techniques: Tearless Trauma, Sneaking up on the Problem, and Chasing the Pain. We'll describe each of these in turn. First we'll review the characteristics that make an event traumatizing, and how these can be distinguished from a nontraumatizing event. We'll also review how the psyche deals with overwhelming trauma in both functional and dysfunctional ways. (See chapter 2 for a full discussion.)

The Four Characteristics of a Traumatic Event

What distinguishes a traumatic from a nontraumatic event? There are several definitions, but there are four characteristics to watch for as you examine your life history and the life histories of your clients. If one of these four conditions is met, the psyche may encode the memory as a traumatic event. The event must:

- Be a perceived threat to physical survival.
- Overwhelm coping capacity, producing a sense of powerlessness.
- Produce a feeling of isolation, aloneness.
- Violate expectations.

Let's examine each in turn, starting with a perceived threat to survival. Some threats to survival are actual. If you're in a serious car accident, you experience an actual threat to your physical survival, and the possibility of death. If you're assaulted by a mugger brandishing a gun, you are faced with a clear threat to your physical survival. That's not a subjective opinion; it's an objective reality.

Such actual and *objective* threats to our physical survival are few and far between. We might experience one serious car accident in an entire lifetime, or one brush with an assailant wielding a weapon. Most of us will not have even a single such experience our entire lives. Yet we might have many *subjective* experiences that we perceive as threats to our survival.

Consider a 4-year-old girl whose father is a morose unemployed alcoholic and whose mother is a violent rage-aholic. The mother screams at the father regularly, and occasionally pummels him with her fists. Each fight drives him deeper into depression. One night the child is awakened by the sound of her parents fighting in the kitchen. She leaves her room and peeks around the edge of the kitchen door. Her mother is brandishing a knife at her father. Her mother catches sight of her. She turns toward the girl and transfers the target of her wrath to the child. "Get out of here or I'll kill you," she shrieks.

As you read this story (a variant of many similar stories told by participants at EFT workshops), you probably don't believe that the mother is really going to murder the child. Yet the child doesn't necessarily know that at the time. With adult judgment, you can interpret the mother's words figuratively. A child will often take them literally. The child does not know that the mother is not speaking literally, and is unlikely to carry out her threat. The child is likely to perceive the event as a threat to her physical survival, the first of the four characteristics of traumatizing events.

The second characteristic of a traumatizing event is that it overwhelms our coping capacity, producing a sense of powerlessness. A female therapist at an EFT workshop recounted that when she was 8 years old, her mother suddenly disappeared. Her father never provided an explanation. One day her mother was living with them, the next day she was not.

Shortly after this, her father remarried. At first she was delighted to have a stepmother, but her joy was short-lived. She soon discovered that her stepmother resented her. She behaved coldly toward the girl. One day when the daughter came home from school, her stepmother gave her a hard shove and said, "Leave this house! You don't belong here any more!" The distraught girl ran crying to her room, and when her father came home, told him what happened. His response? "You shouldn't have provoked your stepmother."

Consider how this type of experience fits the last three criteria for traumatic events. The girl took the most appropriate course of action possible by telling her father what had happened. That's the way she tried to cope with the assault and threat. Her father's response—to blame her—overwhelmed the coping capacity of an 8-year-old, who then felt powerless. She felt isolated and alone in her suffering, the third characteristic of traumatic events.

The experience also violated her expectations, the fourth characteristic. Children naturally have the expectation that they will be protected and nurtured by their parents. When a parent harms the child instead, or consents to or ignores harm being done to the child by someone else, this behavior violates the child's expectations.

Some people have the resilience to cope with extreme events, like rape or beating. Others are traumatized by what might appear to be a minor event. EFT Universe trainer Alina Frank provides this example: "Your mother is preparing a particularly stressful holiday meal, you are 4 years old and wanting her attention. You tug on her apron, but rather than her picking you up as usual, instead, for the first time ever, she unexpectedly turns and yells at you and sends you to bed without dinner. In that moment, all four of the criteria for trauma have been met. Had this happened to you as a 10-year-old, you may have successfully navigated sneaking back into the kitchen, getting some food, and talking it out with your sister. You may have then comforted yourself by playing a video game. With increasing age, resourcing for yourself typically includes a greater variety of options and strategies that reduce the odds of a life challenge becoming a trauma" (Frank, personal communication, 2013). But at the earlier age, without those resources, you're unable to cope. The crucial factor is not how traumatic an event appears to an observer, but the way it is interpreted by the person experiencing the event.

As discussed in chapter 2, even the withdrawal of parental attention can traumatize a child. Infants have an inbred expectation that they will receive emotional connection from their caretakers, and when this is absent, their expectations are violated.

EFT Universe trainer and social worker Tracey Middleton, LCSW, says, "I have had countless clients say, 'I had a great childhood! Nobody ever beat me, nobody ever cussed at me, I was in a wealthy family, had good food, the finest schools money can by, and the best parents in the world, yet I don't love myself, I don't feel like enough, and I believe I am not lovable." As she patiently traces this back to early childhood memories, she often finds a withdrawal of attention on the part of the client's parents.

She says, "We need to train our ears to look for the subtle trauma that comes from an emotional environment that does not meet our most basic needs of being seen, heard, and understood, being loved consistently, with parents who are compassionately present and engaged. In therapy sessions, it's like an archeological dig to uncover a tomb. You get the brushes out and start sweeping little by little to arrive eventually at a pyramid that was dug out of a mountain. It includes all those games Dad missed (even though he bought me the best shoes and uniform), all the nights Mom was consumed by her work and didn't notice I came home with a black eye, and all the time with the maid who raised us because Mom and Dad were off making a million dollars. This leaves the child with limiting beliefs about self and the world, even though there may be few or no events that the client can point to as obviously traumatic. The client concludes that he or she isn't lovable, others can't be trusted, and the world isn't a safe place. Children develop a sense of self-esteem based on how others treat them.

"One client reported that it was very traumatizing when her parents would not talk with her when they were upset at each other. They withheld their love because they were preoccupied with anger. She interpreted their behavior to mean that, 'It is my fault Mom and Dad are not talking. I am a bad girl. There must be something wrong with me.' With countless events of her parents withholding their love when they were upset, she grew up with low self-esteem" (Middleton, personal communication, 2013).

The Trauma Capsule

Now retired, neurologist Robert Scaer, MD, was the medical director of a multidisciplinary pain clinic for 30 years. He estimated that 60% of his pain patients had been abused as children, and virtually all of them were depressed (Scaer, 2012). He identifies the ways in which children, with their limited resources, deal with early life trauma by encapsulating it. Putting a barrier around the event and dissociating from it is often the most useful and adaptive response the child can come up with. As noted in chapter 2, Scaer calls this the "dissociative capsule" and in Clinical EFT training, we use the term "trauma capsule." The unpleasant memory is wrapped in a protective sheath and buried in the subconscious mind or the body. The whole event is encapsulated in this way, from the beginning to the end.

The child may remember events up to the neutral point of emotional calm before the traumatic event began, and also remember events subsequent to the neutral point at which the traumatic event ended, but nothing in between. Putting bad events into a trauma capsule allows the child to cope with the dysfunctionality of the family.

By the time a child reaches the teenage years, he or she might have formed dozens of these trauma capsules. The teenager might have a vague recollection that bad things happened earlier but can't recall the specifics. Yet the collection of traumatic events has shaped his or her worldview and attachment style.

Cognitive Processing: Shifts and How to Identify Them

Some events, even highly traumatic events, we cope with well. A useful guide to how well an event has been processed is the degree of emotion that is evoked in describing it. When you describe a troubling event from your past but you clearly view it in past tense and don't have a lot of emotional charge attached to it, you've probably reconciled yourself to it. You've digested all the unpleasant feelings you experienced at that time and the event is just a bad memory that no longer evokes strong emotion. You accept it, it's in the past, it no longer stimulates negative emotion, and it's part of your history.

If you still have strong emotion attached to the event, however, this may be an indication that you haven't processed it fully. Once I was doing EFT with a psychiatric nurse in his mid 50s. He described an event in which he "lost the love of my life." He had been in a relationship and the woman had ended it. Crying uncontrollably, he described the last time he saw her. His high degree of distress made me assume the event was very recent, and I asked him when it happened. "Eight years ago," he replied. I did not say anything, but I was surprised that he still had such raw feelings so long after the breakup.

The event was so vivid in his mind that he shifted into present tense when describing it. "She's walking toward the jetway at the airport. I'm standing feeling nothing but stunned regret," he said, tears streaming down his face. His eyes were open but his gaze was focused far away, as he relived the event.

Within the trauma capsule, events are often frozen in time. Each sensory channel, sight, sound, touch, taste, and smell, may be part of the memory. The event may be recalled as though it were happening right now, full of emotional charge (Scaer, 2007). Rather than being recalled as part of the historical past, it's reexperienced as part of the living present.

After EFT sessions, clients often shift from describing the event in the present to describing it in the past. This indicates a cognitive shift. They've now come to terms with the memory, and as well as the SUD level going down, they perceive it through a different cognitive lens. The event is past, and they feel reconciled to it. It no longer evokes high emotion.

This phenomenon has been confirmed by research using EEG (electroencephalogram) technology (Diepold & Goldstein, 2008). The EEG showed that when a client was asked to remember a traumatic event, the memory evoked the brain-wave patterns associated with fear and distress. These normalized after a tapping session. Weeks later, when the client again recalled the event, brain patterns remained normal, indicating the permanent resolution of emotional distress.

Tapping on an unprocessed trauma can bring a cognitive shift toward feelings of being at peace, of having moved on, of being safe. As discussed in chapter 2, the client may now imagine her or himself as a spectator witnessing the traumatizing event, rather than a participant. A memory that was vivid may become fuzzy, or the reverse; a fuzzy memory may come into sharp focus. A client may also shift from a victim perspective to feeling compassion for the perpetrator.

All these are indications of cognitive shifts, and the observant EFT practitioner is alert to noticing them. The signal of a client shifting from present to past tense, or shifting from unfocused to vivid visual recall, is more subtle than the SUD rating but can be very revealing. When a client feels safe and describes an event in the past tense, without emotional charge, with a sense of perspective, perhaps even humor, it's likely that the trauma capsule has been successfully dissolved and its contents processed.

When working on a memory that takes the form of a trauma capsule, it's also important to tap on each aspect within the capsule. There might be several peaks of negative emotion within a single brief event.

Imagine an event in which a client called David remembers being bullied in second grade. The bullies pushed the little David into the ground, breaking one of his teeth. Being a careful EFT practitioner, you search for emotional peaks as David tells you the story. You located the start of the story, when he was walking happily home from school, and his SUD level is 0 as he describes it during the session. The end of the story is after he gets home and is safe. You use EFT's Tell the Story Technique and David describes how the event unfolded.

The first emotional peak within the trauma capsule is when David saw the bullies walking in the opposite direction. As he recalls the event today in your office, he's a 7 for that segment of the trauma. They didn't see him at first, and he thought he had escaped. Then they noticed him and crossed the street to accost him. His SUD level shoots up to 10 as he remembers realizing that a confrontation was inevitable. That's the second emotional peak. The bullies taunted him, shoved him to the pavement, and broke his tooth. When David today recalls the taste of blood in his mouth, he's a 7 for that aspect of the experience, the third emotional peak. He went home after that and he remembers his mother comforting him. At the end of the story and the trauma capsule, his SUD score is again 0.

Figure 1 plots each segment of David's EFT coaching session. Time is on the horizontal axis and the SUD rating is the vertical axis. The bulge just after the start of the trauma capsule is the first emotional crescendo (seeing the bullies), the middle bulge is the second emotional

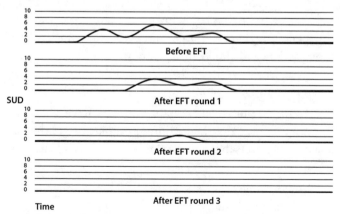

Figure 1. Clearing the trauma capsule with the Tell the Story or Movie Technique.

peak (certainty of confrontation), and the final bulge is the aspect of tasting blood in his mouth.

You incorporate the first emotional peak into a Setup Statement, and tap on "Even though I saw the bullies, I deeply and completely accept myself." It may take several rounds of EFT, including the 9 Gamut Procedure, but eventually David's SUD on that segment of the trauma capsule goes to a 0.

You have him retell the story from the beginning till his SUD score peaks again. You incorporate the new aspect of the traumatic event in a Setup Statement: "Even though I knew confrontation was inevitable when they walked toward me, I deeply and completely accept myself." After you tap, you test your results and keep processing that aspect of the story till David's SUD level is 0 or at least a low number, 1 or 2.

David tells the story again, starting at the neutral phase at the beginning. This time you incorporate the third emotional crescendo into a Setup Statement: "Even thought I tasted blood in my mouth, I deeply and completely accept myself." The SUD level drops to a 0 after a single round of tapping.

To further test your results, you now have David tell the story again from the beginning. If he can get through it without going above a 2, you know you've cleared the trauma capsule.

You don't always have to go to a 0 for every emotional crescendo. I've noticed that I'll leave a client at a 2 for the highest peak, and then when I follow up an hour later or a day later, they're at a 0 for the whole event. Also, when the SUD score for one emotional peak goes down, the SUD scores for the others might drop too. In s 1, you can see that the SUD level for the second emotional peak drops after the first emotional peak is zeroed out. This is due to the generalization effect noted frequently in EFT; when you clear a trauma, associated traumas tend to reduce in intensity, even though you haven't worked directly on them.

EFT's Tell the Story Technique and Movie Technique (having the client silently run the story in his or her head) are the basic and most essential of the Clinical EFT techniques to learn, because they force the practitioner to apply all of the core concepts to the session. Identifying a movie makes certain you pick a specific event.

Checking the SUD level for each part of the traumatic memory ensures that you identify and clear each aspect contained in the trauma capsule. Getting the SUD rating at each junction forces you to test your work frequently. Telling the story all the way through at the end ensures that all the aspects have been dealt with and the trauma capsule has been completely cleared.

Though there are many useful techniques in the body of methods included in Clinical EFT, the Movie Technique and Tell the Story are ones you will return to again and again.

Dissociation

At one EFT workshop, we tested participant levels of emotional trauma before and after tapping. We used a questionnaire called the PCL, short for PTSD Checklist (Blanchard, Jones-Alexander, Buckley, & Forneris, 1996). Everyone's scores on the PCL went down after the workshop, except for two people, whose scores went up. One was a male therapist in his 50s, the other a female director of a psychiatric clinic in her 50s. They felt that they had made big emotional breakthroughs in the workshop, and they were both very pleased with their results after EFT. Why did their traumatic stress scores go up?

The reason is that both of them had a history of dissociation. They had both experienced severe psychological trauma as children, and to cope with the abuse, they'd distanced themselves from their feelings.

As with forming a trauma capsule, the dissociative response makes perfect sense for a child (see chapter 2 for a full discussion). The child has to survive and live on in the abusive situation. He or she cannot escape, and the caregiver is often the abuser. The child resolves this paradox by pushing the bad experiences out of consciousness and into the subconscious mind. Carl Jung described the "shadow," that part of the self into which these "unacceptable" or unhealed traumas are stuffed. Poet Robert Bly calls it "the bag," and he says that we fill our bags with these unhealed experiences during childhood and drag the bag through our adult life like a huge burden that weighs us down and robs us of our joy.

After a lifetime spent stuffing bad experiences into one's shadow, or forming trauma capsules, and not truly feeling or processing negative experiences, a person can develop a reflexive habit of responding to negative experiences this way. Such a person might feel very few of their feelings deeply, and perceive emotions as dangerous and disruptive. Their safety lies in dissociating.

When a person with a long history of using dissociation as a coping strategy and with a huge collection of disowned personality fragments stuffed into their shadow starts to learn EFT, these fragments may begin to emerge. Although the person might have managed to feel okay in the past by suppressing these fragments and associated feelings, and might have reported low emotional intensity, they're now feeling them fully, and reporting high emotional intensity. In this case, a rise in emotional intensity is actually a sign of healing, as long as the emotion is then fully processed, to the point at which the intensity subsides and the shadow fragment is reintegrated into the whole personality as an acceptable part.

Inducing Dissociation

Dissociation can be a useful therapeutic tool. When remembering an event is so terrifying to a client that thinking about it is impossible without fear, healing might be impossible unless some dissociation takes place. In these cases, dissociation can be deliberately induced as an interim measure to help a client approach the possibility of healing. EFT's Tearless Trauma Technique makes use of dissociation in this way. It gives the client permission to dissociate as far as is required by the traumatic memory in order to start the healing journey. Once some progress has been made, part of the dissociative barrier can be removed and, with the client's permission, another layer of healing can be attempted.

Scaer (2012) believes that several elements of EFT are effective for dealing with dissociation. These include the ritualistic nature of the affirmations used in the Setup Statement, which may anchor a client to reality even when the client tends to dissociate, and the integration of the functions of the left and right hemispheres of the brain through the 9 Gamut Procedure. My own experience with EFT is that the 9 Gamut is essential in cases of childhood trauma, which, as we have seen, is a factor for the majority of clients.

The Gentle Techniques give a client permission to dissociate temporarily as part of the healing process. With tapping, distress usually diminishes and, eventually, the feared event can be faced head on. The Tearless Trauma Technique erects mental barriers between the client and the fearful memory. Several layers of these dissociative barriers might be required before the client feels safe enough to start tapping on the event. The practitioner can induce this type of dissociation, suggest layer after layer until the client feels enough security to begin the work of healing. The following section explains how to perform the Tearless Trauma Technique.

Tearless Trauma Technique

1. Ask your client to choose a specific traumatic incident from the past to work on. For example, the client might say, "I almost drowned after my angry older brother threw me off the boat into the lake when I

was 6." The phrase "My brother tormented me" is too general because the abuse may have occurred over the course of numerous incidents.

2. Ask your client to estimate (on the SUD scale of 0 to 10, with 10 being the most intense) what the emotional intensity would be if they were to imagine the incident. Tell them not to imagine it, but simply to guess what the intensity would be if they did. This estimate is useful, while allowing the client to avoid the emotional pain inherent in full memory. Write down the client's estimate. Make sure the client's eyes remain open, so they can see they're in a safe place. The way memory works is that we combine cues from the environment around us now with the old memory from the past. Keeping the eyes open during traumatic recall associates the safety of the present moment with the trauma encoded in the memory.

3. Suggest an innocuous reminder phrase such as "the incident at the lake" that allows a layer of dissociation from the terror experienced in nearly drowning. Incorporate the phrase into EFT's Setup Statement and do a round of tapping. Avoid general statements like "brother torment" because it is so broad that it could refer to dozens of other events. Make sure the phrase is not too provocative, such as "the bloody knife."

4. After the round, ask the client to estimate again what the intensity would be if the client were to imagine the incident. Compare that rating to the original one. It is usually a significantly lower number.

5. Do more rounds of EFT, with new intensity estimates between each one. Three or four rounds bring most clients' estimates down to between 0 and 3.

6. When the client's guess has dropped to an acceptably low rating, do another round of tapping. Ask them to imagine the incident itself. Note that this is the first time you have requested them to do so (prior to this you only asked them to guess at the emotional intensity they would experience were they to imagine the incident). Now ask the client to rate the emotional intensity of the incident. Most people go to 0, but if your client does not, address the remaining aspects of the incident with the Movie Technique or Tell the Story Technique.

The Tearless Trauma Technique can be used in any case that involves trauma. It can be used with both groups and individuals. If your client has experienced abuse as a child, war, rape, torture, or other traumatic events, it's a good place to start an EFT session.

In the following article, Australian therapist Steve Wells reports on his success the first time he tried using the Tearless Trauma Technique with a group. Participants were startled at how effective it was, even though they weren't receiving individual counseling.

Using the Tearless Trauma Technique in a Group

By Steve Wells

I just spent the weekend presenting a personal development seminar incorporating EFT and other energy therapy techniques. I tried out the Tearless Trauma Technique.

Sixteen people were asked to guess their SUD score when guessing the intensity of their trauma initially. All of them reported being between 8 and 10. Eleven went to 0 or near 0 after four rounds of tapping when asked to vividly reimagine the traumatic incident. The others were all at 4–5, and two more rounds took care of most of this. I offered to help during the break one woman whose SUD level remained at a 4, but she came up and told me she really saw how she could get beyond this herself and wanted to do so, as she felt empowered by the technique.

Most of the participants were absolutely astounded when they tried to reaccess the feelings and weren't able to. The most outstanding result, however, was by one gentleman who reported that an incredible feeling of sadness he'd been experiencing almost his whole life regarding his father was absolutely gone and he was now experiencing a feeling of complete peace. You should have seen the way his face shone. This guy had previously had a taste of EFT in another seminar I had run. He came to this one because after he used EFT to deal with his constant anger and anxiety, his wife said it was like getting a new husband. Needless to say, she was *very* happy for him to come and do more.

❖ ❖ ❖

Further Layers of Therapeutic Dissociation

There are many traumatic events for which this single layer of dissociation—asking a client to guess at what the SUD score might be if the event were imagined—does not provide a safe enough distance from the event. A massage therapist at an EFT workshop wanted to dispel her fear of public speaking. She came up to work with me in front of the group, but I quickly noticed she was making little progress. Inquiry revealed that having her session watched by other people triggered her, so we turned her chair so her back was to the other workshop participants, which made her more comfortable.

When she tuned in to the body sensations that arose when she imagined making a public speech, she got in touch with a long-forgotten childhood memory. An uncle of hers had exposed himself to her when she was about 2 years old. She could not bear to think of the event.

We used a further layer of dissociation by having her lock the event in a box. It was a yellow box with 10 padlocks holding it shut. Even then, thinking about the yellow box took her SUD level "through the roof." She decided to put the box inside a safe on an island in the middle of the ocean. Contemplating the island, her SUD level was a 9. Tapping quickly brought that to a 0, and she opened the safe. Her SUD looking at the box was back at a 9, but EFT quickly brought it down to a 1. We then used the Movie Technique, and she imagined the movie playing inside the box. Her SUD level went back to a 10 and we tapped till it was again a 1.

Not until she was ready and willing to open the box did we work on the movie. When she opened the box, the intensity of the movie was only a 6, and it quickly went down to a 1. The intensity of the images faded, indicating a cognitive shift.

I decided to test our results by having her turn to the group and give an impromptu public speech. She was happy to do this. She then stood up on a chair and continued speaking, laughing and waving her hands around as she expressed delight at her newfound emotional freedom.

Layers of dissociation, with the movie playing behind a curtain, or in a locked movie theater, or placing the movie theater inside a box, allow a client to diminish the intensity of a traumatic memory gradually. I've even had clients decide to place the box on a distant planet. That's as close as they can get to the personal tragedy locked inside. It usually surprises me how quickly they can retrieve the box, open it, and watch the movie.

The safety that the Tearless Trauma Technique provides is key to allowing such rapid resolution of deeply disturbing events. Good EFT practitioners let clients proceed at their own pace, never pushing them to confront events that might overwhelm their coping capacity, and allowing them enough layers of dissociation and sufficient time to confront the event gradually. Practitioners sometimes have clients put the traumatic event back in the box for more tapping in the next session, or put the box back in the safe, or on the island, in order to provide the client with the assurance of safety between EFT sessions.

Exceptions to the Rule of Being Specific

The Tearless Trauma Technique presents an exception to the rule of being specific. The Basic Recipe instructs you to find a specific memory to work on. When the memory is too traumatic to contemplate, it's useful to dissociate, and it can also be useful to make general statements like "the lake incident." There are some other exceptions to the rule of being specific.

One is in cases of excessive emotional intensity. If a client is crying uncontrollably, it is wise to pull back from the specifics of the event and tap on general statements like "abandonment" or "misery." I sometimes use a very general statement such as "Even though bad things happened, I deeply and completely accept myself." The reason for the rule of being specific is to get clients in touch with their emotions. If they're crying, they're very much in touch with those emotions, and forcing them to remember traumatizing details of the event is counterproductive, risking the possibility of emotional flooding and retraumatization. My experience is that such clients remain very much in touch with their emotions even when the practitioner backs off from being specific.

Another exception to the rule of being specific is when a client has many similar events in his or her past, and you'd like to reduce the intensity of all of them simultaneously. For instance, a man who was beaten repeatedly by his father might find remembering a particular beating too upsetting. In this case, tapping on the general heading of "the beatings" might allow the intensity of the whole collection of beatings to diminish, especially if you use a method like the 9 Gamut technique, which experience shows can clear many similar emotional traumas simultaneously.

Sneaking Up on the Problem

Sneaking Up on the Problem is the second of EFT's Gentle Techniques. It's very simple yet effective. It's often used to address hopelessness, catastrophizing, resistance, and core beliefs that the problem cannot be solved. Examples of these core beliefs are:

I'm not lovable.

I'll never get over this problem.

Everyone in my family is like this.

Nothing I've tried has worked.

EFT isn't going to be able to fix this.

My pain will never go away.

Relationships aren't safe.

The doctor says my symptoms will get worse.

No one in my family has ever changed.

Working on this is hopeless.

I don't know where to start.

I've always been this way and always will be.

Such negative cognitions can also take the form of clichés, such as:

It's a dog-eat-dog world.

The apple never falls far from the tree.

No pain, no gain.

The higher you rise, the harder you fall.

Statements like these are not a promising start to a course of personal transformation! Yet while most of us have problems we've been able to solve, we also have problems that have defied our best efforts at solution. Perhaps everyone in your family is overweight. Perhaps no one in your family has ever gone to college. Perhaps your pain has never gone away before. Most people have a collection of issues that have not budged despite their best efforts over many years, and they may have no belief that change is possible. Nothing in their prior experience suggests it is, and they bring this mindset to an EFT session.

Sneaking Up on the Problem is a simple and elegant technique for dealing with these unhelpful beliefs and resistance. The practitioner simply agrees with the client! You incorporate the client's exact words into a Setup Statement, bracketing them with "Even though…" and "I deeply and completely accept myself." For instance, the client says, "I can never lose weight no matter how hard I try." The practitioner sneaks up on the problem by tapping with the client while affirming, "Even though I can never lose weight no matter how hard I try, I deeply and completely accept myself."

Clients are usually surprised or baffled that the practitioner is not attempting to talk them out of their negative belief. This technique is powerful because it acknowledges clients exactly where they are, not attempting to change them. The great client-centered therapist Carl Rogers said that the paradox of therapy is that the first step in transformation is accepting yourself just where you are (Rogers, 1957). EFT uses this observation to therapeutic advantage, by including even the most negative of cognitions in a Setup Statement. This both validates the client and opens the gateway of change. In my experience, these beliefs shift after just one or two rounds of tapping.

The Sneaking Up technique is also useful when a client states categorically that he or she is unable to remember specific events. You'll ask for one and the client may make a general statement like "I can never remember any specific events." You then build this into the Setup Statement, "Even though I can never remember any specific events, I deeply and completely accept myself." It's uncanny to observe how this use of Sneaking Up is usually followed by a client saying, "Something just popped into my head," after which he or she recounts a specific event.

Another common response is "This probably has nothing to do with my problem, but I just remembered…" and the client goes on to describe an event that is key to solving the presenting problem. Sneaking Up seems to somehow change the client's sense of reality, broadening the scope of possibilities to include the element of healing.

It's also very easy to do, requiring no skill or insight on the part of the practitioner. The practitioner simply incorporates the client's exact words into a Setup Statement. There are occasional junctures in therapy when even the best therapist is stumped and can't decide where to go next. Sneaking Up is a good standby in these situations, and usually provides forward momentum to the session.

I took several classes from clinical psychologist Brad Blanton, who was one of the last students of Fritz Perls, the developer of Gestalt therapy. Brad is a brilliant therapist, and one of the ways he would address catastrophizing was to not merely agree with the client, but to take the argument one step further. If a client would say, "The pain will always be with me," Brad might extrapolate with a statement like, "It might even get worse. In fact, it could get worse and worse until you die of pain." This would usually evoke a reaction in the client such as, "Wait a minute, it's not that bad!" One of Brad's favorite sayings, after patiently listening to what he termed a client's "tragic story," was "But wait! It gets worse!" Emphasizing the negative was a way to induce the client to argue for the possibility of positive change (Blanton, 2005).

This trick can enhance the effect of Sneaking Up. If a client says, "I'll always be sad," sometimes I'll agree, and affirm they'll get sadder. Taken to its logical conclusion, you can say, "Even after you're dead, people will look at the body in the casket and say, 'What a sad corpse.'" This usually produces a gale of laughter from the client, and the spell of the catastrophic trance is broken.

Alina Frank also views Sneaking Up as the outermost in a ring of concentric circles that surround the core of full healing. The outer ring often consists of fear or resistance that your client may have toward working on a traumatic event. By starting off with vague tapping statements such as "Even though I don't want to even think about that bad thing that happened" or "Even though that event was so devastating that EFT could never help me," we can ease the client's fears, establish a safe working relationship, and bring the intensity down sufficiently to allow the next deeper layer to be addressed.

As we move closer to the center, the statements can slowly become more specific, such as "Even though I feel this fear just talking about what happened to me when I was at the lake when I was 6…" Once a client's fears of addressing the event directly have been collapsed, the innermost circle consisting of the actual event may be addressed with the Tell the Story or Movie Technique (Frank, personal communication, 2013).

Chasing the Pain

The third and final of EFT's Gentle Techniques is Chasing the Pain. Often clients have more than one site of pain. There might be a pain in the shoulder rated at a 9, plus a pain in the lower back with a SUD level of 4, along with a sore knee rated at a 2. When Chasing the Pain, the EFT practitioner guides the client on tapping on each site of pain in turn. When the pain at one site goes down to a low SUD score, you tap on the next-highest pain, and on down the line. Clients might also become aware of new pains as old ones are tapped away. After you tap with a client on her sore ankle, which is a 5, she might tell you that the pain has shifted to her hip, which is an 8. You tap on the hip, after which the pain shifts to her stomach, which is a 4. The practitioner follows the client's lead, chasing the pain wherever it occurs.

The reason that Chasing the Pain is considered a Gentle Technique is that many clients use pain as a proxy for emotion. A grizzled veteran who is unable to share any emotions will readily describe his pain. Processing emotional trauma may be too difficult or triggering for a client to contemplate, or carry a stigma, while processing physical pain carries no such meaning. Physical symptoms like pain are thought of as objective medical realities, and few clients are unwilling to share them.

As the experience of Dr. Scaer and many EFT practitioners shows, much physical pain is tied to childhood abuse. Since the abuser was often the client's caregiver, feelings of anger toward the caregiver might be entwined with feelings of love and gratitude. A man might remember being beaten by his father, but also remember being loved and taught useful skills that helped him prosper later in life. Sometimes clients feel that talking about a parent's abuse is disloyal because the parent also loved them and provided for them. At a conscious level, a client may be unwilling to address abuse. Here tapping on pain can serve to dissipate that emotional material without needing to confront it.

Fritz Perls noted the link between physical symptoms and emotions after working with an artist on his repressed anger. The artist was extremely nearsighted. After Gestalt therapy sessions, his many symptoms resolved and his vision normalized. Perls observed: "Particularly if you get a combination of symptoms, like nearsightedness, lower back pain, anger indirectly expressed, instances of sexual impotency—you can have a noticeable positive impact on all the symptoms at once....[P]sychologically the overruling of the taboos against expressiveness allows for greater self-expression, particularly of anger, then the eyesight improves, anger decreases, back pain goes away and sexual function is restored" (Blanton, 2011).

For some clients, pain offers a useful proxy for emotions. As pain after pain is tapped away using the Chasing the Pain technique, it is likely that a client unable to face his or her emotional trauma is making progress on resolving it in a way that is safe and non-triggering.

Sneaking Away from the Problem

Sneaking Away from the Problem is a technique for concluding an EFT session when it's apparent that the work is incomplete. One of the problematic issues in psychotherapy sessions is that a client is often feeling upset at the end of the appointment. A session might uncover major issues, but when the hour is at an end, they have not been resolved. One client said, "The end of some of my sessions with my therapist are like being on the operating table getting open heart surgery. Suddenly, the surgeon looks at his watch and says, 'Oops, time for the next patient. Sorry there wasn't time to finish the operation. We'll sew you up and get to you later.' I feel like I'm bleeding on the gurney. I leave my therapist's office crying, confused, upset, unable to function for hours afterwards."

Sneaking Away is a method of using EFT to name and describe this problem in such a manner that a client's process is honored, and affirming that there will be time later on to address the problem fully. Tapping and using Sneaking Away gives a client a sense of completion. Examples of Sneaking Away affirmations are:

Even though I still feel terrible, there will be time to work on this later.

Even though I've just started to get in touch with this issue, I'll be fine.

We'll put the problem back in the box, behind the movie curtain, till next session.

Even though I didn't solve all of this problem today, there's time in the future.

There's plenty of time for me to heal. I don't have to do it all today.

This problem has been here for a long time, and what I've done today is enough.

I don't have to demand from myself that I heal fully today.

I can put this away and pick it up next time.

There's always time and space for me to work on this.

Even though I'm really triggered right now, I can manage till next time.

In my experience, affirmations of Sneaking Away are enormously comforting to the client. Tapping and saying statements like this usually reduce SUD levels rapidly. Occasionally in practice sessions in EFT workshops, when I'm observing participants working with each other, time for the exercise will be up, but one person is still a

10. Sneaking Away usually quickly reduces that to a 1 or 2, after which the participant can go on with the learning process of the workshop.

Sneaking Away can also be used to address the "doorknob effect," in which a client recalls a painful event when he or she is about to leave the session (Middleton, personal communication, 2013). This may reflect two contradictory urges present simultaneously in the client's awareness. One urge is to bring the issue to light by discussing it with the therapist. The second urge is to not discuss it because it is so traumatic. Unconsciously, the client resolves this dilemma by surfacing the issue at a time when it is impossible to process through to resolution. Sneaking Away can be used to sidestep the dilemma with which the client has presented the therapist. Tapping on a phrase such as, "Even though there's no time to address this now, I'm safe till our next session, and we can talk about it then," honors both of the mutually exclusive voices competing for the client's attention.

Touch and Breathe (TAB)

Touch and Breathe, abbreviated as TAB, is a development of TFT that is sometimes used in EFT as well. Developed by TFT practitioners in the 1990s (Diepold, 2000), it is the same as Clinical EFT, except that it does not use tapping. Instead, it uses a light fingertip touch on each acupoint accompanied by a breath. It is described in the book *The Energy of Belief* (Bender & Sise, 2007).

The indications for using TAB are when a client is uncomfortable with tapping. For instance, a rape victim in one workshop I offered was triggered by the tapping itself. The percussive nature of tapping on her body reminded her of the rape. So we used TABbing instead. Tabbing and tapping can be equally successful at reducing SUD scores.

Another EFT practitioner had a new female client, whom we'll call Jane, who was an Iraq veteran. After deployment, Jane had developed a slew of symptoms including multiple chemical sensitivities. This is a condition in which many substances common in the environment, such as soap and plastic, produce an allergic reaction. Jane's skin had become so sensitive that she could not tolerate wearing regular clothes, or constriction of any kind around her body. All she was able to wear were sack-like microfiber dresses of a certain brand. In her first session, Jane was unable to tolerate tapping on even a single acupressure point. The practitioner used tabbing instead of tapping.

By the end of the first session, Jane was able to comfortably tap on her collarbone point, using TAB for the other points instead. Midway through the second session, she was able to tolerate tapping on all the points. She also quickly lost her sensitivities and, after six EFT sessions, Jane's PTSD symptoms had normalized.

Posttraumatic Growth

While PTSD grabs the headlines, it's worth noting that terrible experiences can also produce posttraumatic growth. This is the phenomenon of people becoming stronger and more resilient in the wake of traumatic events (Tedeschi & Calhoun, 2004). PTSD is not inevitable. Roughly one third of veterans returning from Iraq and Afghanistan will develop PTSD, but two thirds will not (Tanielian & Jaycox, 2008). Research has shown a correlation between negative childhood events and the development of adult PTSD (Ozer, Best, Lipsey, & Weiss, 2008). Yet some people emerge from miserable childhoods stronger and more resilient than their peers.

Adversity can sometimes make us even stronger than we might have been had we not suffered it. New research is showing that people who experience a traumatic event but are then able to process and integrate the experience are more resilient than those who don't experience such an event (Stanley & Jha, 2009).

A model developed by former General Loree Sutton, MD, former commanding officer of the Defense Center for Excellence and other authorities shows that such people are even better prepared for future adversity, and research that will be published in the coming years will confirm the value of posttraumatic resilience (Sutton, 2013). The way this works in your body's nervous system is that when you're exposed to a stress and successfully re-regulate yourself, you increase the neural connections associated with handling trauma. Neural plasticity (or neuroplasticity), the phenomenon that we build new neural connections in nerve circuits we use frequently, works in your favor. You increase the size of the signaling pathways in your nervous system that handle recovery from stress. These larger and improved signaling pathways equip you to better handle future stress, making you more resilient in the face of life's upsets and problems.

Posttraumatic growth has only recently been named and identified, and has not yet received the research attention that PTSD has received. I believe that using EFT soon after traumatic events increases the likelihood that a person will be able to make positive meaning out of tragedy, and build the neural circuits required to handle future adversity. I also believe it's possible that further research will show that the events that trigger PTSD can later be reimagined with tapping in a way that promotes posttraumatic growth and generates growth in the neural networks that regulate stress.

One of the most provocative studies I was involved with looked at the experience of 218 veterans and their spouses (Church & Brooks, 2014). They attended a weeklong workshop that included 4 days of EFT and other energy psychology techniques. As noted in chapter 2, when they began, 83% of the veterans and 29% of the spouses tested positive for PTSD. After the retreat, these numbers had dropped dramatically. When they were retested 6 weeks later, only 28% of the veterans and only 4% of the spouses had PTSD. This represents a significant drop in their symptoms. It's also possible to see the results as a gateway to a new set of possibilities for veterans and their spouses. Human potential that was circumscribed by suffering might be unleashed after liberation from that suffering. EFT can be used as a way to tip the balance after tragedy, away from PTSD and toward posttraumatic growth.

Improving
EFT's Effectiveness

Those who are new to EFT often ask when and how frequently they should practice tapping. The answer is: as often as you like—or, better yet, as often as possible. EFT is very flexible and forgiving. The more often you practice, however, the sooner EFT becomes a familiar tool that you can use without effort. The more you use it, the better it works. The more you use it, the more likely you are to remember to use it when you really need it.

I usually recommend that you start by tapping as soon as you wake up in the morning, before every meal, and before falling asleep at night.

That's five times a day right there. Tap whenever you use the bathroom or take a shower and you'll add a few more. Some people tap whenever they come to a stop sign or red light. Quite a few tap while they walk. You don't have to do the entire Basic Recipe; just a few quick taps as time permits will help reduce stressful emotions. Then, as soon as you have enough time, follow up with the complete Sequence.

Many people tap before, during, or after they pray or meditate. EFT tapping can improve any project or activity.

When you're in a hurry, try tapping on a single point, such as the Karate Chop point, while you focus on your pain or problem. Just that can produce good results. In addition, if you get in the habit of tapping on the EFT acupoints without reciting a Setup or focusing your thoughts on anything specific, that alone will help keep your emotions balanced and help you live a happier life.

Try tapping to music. This is a popular activity in some EFT workshops. It keeps the group focused and energetic, and it's an easy way to avoid an energy slump in the afternoon. Teaching children to tap to music is a great way to introduce them to EFT. Tap at whatever rhythm feels right. Experiment with classical music, rock, ballads, rap, opera, marches, movie soundtracks, or whatever you most enjoy.

Tap while you read your e-mail or work at the computer. Tap while you watch TV. Tap while you talk on the phone. Tap while you study; that's an easy way to improve your reading comprehension and recall. Tap right now as you read this page.

If you tap while you describe things that you've seen or experienced, your recollections are more likely to be accurate. In fact, EFT would probably significantly improve the accuracy of eyewitness testimony. In EFT, we use the Tell the Story, Watch the Movie, and Tearless Trauma Techniques (see chapters 3 and 6) to help people describe difficult events without feeling emotionally over-whelmed. With their emotions under control, they are able to think, remember, and process information more efficiently. EFT practitioners have reported on tapping's incredible calming effect when applied immediately after an accident, tragedy, or disaster.

Here's a great tip from EFT practitioner Rick Wilkes. It has special application for those experiencing PTSD because it offers a method for dealing with underlying issues easily and automatically, without conscious effort. Many have found that their way of looking at a situation changes as a result of following Rick's simple instructions.

The Tap-While-You-Gripe Technique
by Rick Wilkes

Have you ever called a friend just to gripe about everything that's gone wrong in your day? The truth is that when things go wrong, we need to feel that we're not alone. So we turn to trusted friends and family to let off steam and be comforted. It's a natural part of being human. Most of us have been expressing our pain this way since we were very young children.

What I call "griping" is just a way to retell a story with emotional intensity. And there is scientific proof that this can help us. Recent brain studies show that there's an *opportunity* when we relive an experience to have the stored emotions of that experience heal, or become even more intense. As we recall the story and feel the emotions in our body, our brain is making a decision—one that can go either way!

That is why I suggest that you always tap while you gripe. Tap while you complain. Tap every time you tell a story that has negative emotional intensity. Pretty soon, you'll probably notice you have a lot less in your life to gripe about!

Here's how you can get started:

You've had a bad day. You want to feel that there's someone out there that understands you, that cares about you, that takes your side. So you pick up the phone, and you call your best friend. Start tapping, and tap continuously while you talk to her!

(Karate Chop): [Ring…Ring…] *Hello?*

(Top of Head): *Oh, I'm so glad I reached you.*

(Inside Eyebrow): *I have had such a terrible day!*

(Side of Eye): *I really need someone to talk to.*

(Under Eye): *Do you have a few minutes?*

(Under Nose): *First off, this *e3^+$ boss of mine…*

(Then Chin, Collarbone, Under the Arm, Karate Chop, and back to Top of Head, etc.)

The order of the points doesn't matter. The number of taps at each point doesn't matter. You can tap one point that feels good the whole call if you want. You can use the finger points. Just tap continuously while you talk. Don't stop!

Why would we do this? We talk to others to feel better, don't we? But there are two approaches to griping and complaining. The first is, alas, the more common. It is to gather people to our side in the upcoming war. We tell a story to make us "right" and the other party "wrong." With this plan, we must build intensity in ourselves and in others while we plan revenge (or a lawsuit, divorce, or other dramatic action designed so we win and the other loses).

The other approach is to want to heal from an emotional pain. We're mature enough to know that intensifying the fear by making us the "Victim" and others into the "Powerful Force of True Evil" just creates war inside us, not peace.

We can make our healing far more likely if we tap the acupoints while we express our hurt and our anger and our sadness and our feelings of being out of control. We use what has been human nature since cave folks sat around the fire—the need to tell our story to tribe members to gain their supportive energy—and we use that supportive energy in a new way that is far more likely to result in a sense of peace for all of us.

What I find is that tapping while I gripe and complain shifts my entire perspective. As the noise of the emotional disruption settles down, I am far more likely to hear my intuition guide me to steps that resolve the situation in the best possible way.

Try it for yourself. Tap the acupoints while you are on the phone. No one needs to know that you are tapping. And just notice whether you see a change that helps you feel both more peaceful and more empowered. I am confident you will.

In fact, you may find this so effective that you pick up your phone and tap while you gripe without even calling your friend. Once you get it all out of your system, then you dial...and perhaps have a very different kind of conversation.

❊ ❊ ❊

Can You Do EFT Incorrectly?

This is an interesting question. EFT is so forgiving and versatile that finding ways in which it doesn't work can be a challenge. In fact, many people who use EFT declare that the only way to do it wrong is not to use it.

You can do an incomplete EFT treatment (which will make more sense as we explore advanced concepts), but if you combine focused thought and intention with tapping, your efforts will probably work no matter what Setup Statement or tapping sequence you use.

For example, you can omit the words "Even though" and simply state the problem:

My back hurts.

I can't sleep through the night.

I'm upset.

And you don't have to tap on the EFT acupoints in any specific order. I recommend the Sequence described in the Basic Recipe because it's easy to remember, but you can tap the points in any order, on either side or on both sides, or from top to bottom or bottom to top, and you'll still get good results. If your intention is to treat a specific issue and you combine that intention with any type of acupoint stimulation, you are likely to get results. That said, however, the results documented in research on EFT are based on application of the Basic Recipe in its standard form.

Note that you need not worry about tapping on too many points. The beauty of meridian therapies is that when you stimulate points that you don't need, you don't hurt yourself or cause complications—and when you tap on points that you do need, the process works.

The 9 Gamut Procedure (see appendix), which in the early days of EFT was a standard part of the protocol, is not always used now. Some people only use it when progress stalls. However, many practitioners consider it essential, especially in cases of trauma.

As you become more practiced in using EFT, you will find what works best for you and your clients. I encourage people to discover their own personal EFT acupoint and try it first. Most of us, if we pay attention, realize that we're drawn to a certain point, or we notice that every time there is a shift in the way we're feeling while tapping, it's when we're tapping on the same point. For some, it's the Under Eye; for others, it's the Under the Arm or Karate Chop point. If you set out to relieve your back pain and you tap on a single acupoint and the pain goes away, you're done.

If you get your best results by tapping on all the points according to the Basic Recipe protocol, however, by all means continue to do so. The goal is to get the best results possible, in whatever way that occurs for an individual.

Conditions That Interfere

Now let's consider some of the conditions that can interfere with your ability to neutralize traumatic memories and reduce or eliminate the symptoms of PTSD, all of which can be addressed with EFT. In addition to Psychological Reversal, discussed in chapter 3, the following can also interfere.

Self-Talk and the Writings on Your Walls

A potential stumbling block to reaching your goals with EFT is your subconscious mind and its programming, which is reflected by your self-talk, the thoughts and statements having anything to do with you that rattle around in your head at all hours of the day and night.

Your self-talk's programming is known in EFT as the "writings on your walls." This writing contains all of the "rules" you grew up with or absorbed through life experiences—statements you heard as a child that reflect your family or cultural conditioning, or ideas or attitudes, especially about you, that you've absorbed throughout your life. Here are some examples:

Life is dangerous.

You can't be too careful. Everyone has a hidden agenda.

It's all my fault.

I don't deserve to be happy.

It's important to never show weakness.

I'm just not good in relationships.

Tail-Enders

Closely related to the writings on your walls are the tail-enders they inspire. Tail-enders are the "yes, but" statements that pop up when you try to set new goals or write new affirmations.

The most obvious tail-enders are the words you hear in your mind when you try out a new idea. These words often have a sarcastic ring to them: *Yeah, right. When pigs fly. I'll believe that when I see it. You must be kidding. Forget it. No way. Impossible.*

Tail-enders are the nemeses of affirmations. A standard piece of advice in metaphysical circles is to turn negative self-talk around by stating the opposite. For example, if you hear yourself saying, "This is going to be a terrible day," try switching that to "This is a wonderful day." If your conscious and subconscious minds accept the affirmation, it probably will be a wonderful day, but what if they don't? That's when tail-enders create mischief.

Tail-enders can show up at the end of a "Choices" statement, in which you describe your goal, as in this example:

Even though I feel angry all the time, I choose to stay calm and relaxed, no matter who is trying to get me upset...

…but I know that's never going to happen.

…but I've always been this way and it's too hard to change.

…but I can't let people take advantage of me.

…but there are some things I just can't let go of.

…but it's too dangerous to let my guard down.

Whenever you notice a tail-ender, see it for what it is: an important clue that is pointing to core issues. Where did that idea come from? Can you hear someone's voice in your head, like the voice of your mother, father, teacher, neighbor, or friend? What events from long ago come to mind? Every memory or event can be put to good use as a Setup that combines tail-enders with the writings on your walls.

When demonstrating EFT in workshops or when working with clients, EFT practitioners often create "fill in the blank" statements and wait for the person to complete the sentence. For example:

When I think about how important it is not to let people take advantage of me, I remember _____.

When I relax and let my mind drift back to my childhood, I can hear my dad's voice saying, "_____."

Even though I can never forgive _____ for _____…

As soon as a specific memory appears, you can turn it into a Setup:

Even though my dad always said I was an out-of-control hothead, I fully and completely accept myself.

Even though I got in a fight with Eddie Jackson in high school, and my folks said they were giving up on me...

Continue revising the Setup so that it focuses on the person's emotions:

Even though my dad did nothing but criticize and scowl at me, and it really hurt because I could never get his approval no matter how hard I tried, and it made me really mad, in fact it still does, and just the sight of him standing there would turn my stomach, I would like to let go of that unhappy time.

Saying Goodbye to the Past

Another way to release core issues that contribute to self-sabotage is to tap while saying:

Even though _____ happened, it doesn't have to bother me anymore. Even though _____ happened and I can't change the past, I can change my emotional connection to the past. Even though _____ happened, it doesn't have to affect me anymore, I can relax about it and let it go, I can function in the present moment.

When you build on the Basic Recipe by experimenting, trying new approaches, and exploring new ways of presenting and using EFT, you may find your results improving.

How to Tell Whether EFT Is Working

There may be times, however, that you wonder whether your tapping made a difference. When the problem is pain, the test is simple—either the pain goes away or it doesn't. If it does, it's probably because EFT successfully neutralized emotional issues that were contributing factors or an underlying cause of the pain. But pain relief isn't the only indication of EFT's effectiveness. Here are some common signs of EFT at work in a tapping session, no matter the problem or issue addressed.

- **The person sighs.** This often happens after a round of tapping and it reflects an energy shift away from stress toward relaxation.

- **The person yawns.** The yawn may or may not be accompanied by fatigue. Some people have fallen asleep in the middle of their EFT sessions, but even well-rested people yawn during and after tapping.

- **The person's breathing changes.** Most of us breathe shallowly, especially when we're under stress. Longer, slower, deeper breaths are almost always a signal that EFT is working. The more balanced your emotional state, the smoother and more relaxed your breathing.

- **The person's voice changes.** During an EFT session, it's not uncommon for someone's voice to crack, for stress or tension to make the voice actually squeak, or for the person to have trouble talking. Then, after EFT brings the person's emotional state into balance, his or her voice sounds deeper, rounder, fuller, more confident, stronger, and more vibrant. Speech patterns change, too, going from stumbling and inarticulate to clear, coherent, fluid, and eloquent.

- **The person's posture and body language change.** People who are depressed, anxious, frightened, or in pain sit, stand, and walk very differently from the way they do when they're comfortable, confident, relaxed, happy, and healthy. In successful EFT sessions, postural changes are often obvious. Instead of sitting hunched, with the head down and a curved spine, most people straighten up, lift their heads, and look at the world around them.

- **The person cries.** The Tearless Trauma Technique (see chapter 6) is at the heart of EFT, and it really is possible to work through serious problems without weeping. But in many cases, people do cry. Tears are often a sign of release or relief. Even if the tears are a symptom of discomfort, in which case the Tearless Trauma Technique is used to reduce the discomfort level, the emotional change indicates that EFT is working.

- **Sinuses drain.** Congested sinuses that drain suddenly reflect an energy shift in the body.

- **Facial muscles relax.** Actually, muscles all over the body soften, but changes in facial expression, such as from tense and stressed to relaxed and comfortable, are obvious clues that tapping is working. EFT can make such a difference in facial expression that some practitioners call it an instant face-lift. A few rounds of effective tapping can help you look years younger as well as happier.

- **Blood pressure and pulse change.** Often people begin an EFT session in a state of anxiety, with an elevated pulse rate or elevated blood pressure. In those cases, successful EFT tapping—even if it's for something unrelated to the physical symptom—brings both pulse and blood pressure back to normal.

- **The person feels hot or cold.** A temperature change, such as feeling suddenly hot or cold, is another indication that EFT is working. A small or large area of back pain may feel intensely warm or hot, and the pain may pulse or vibrate. Someone who feels suddenly hot may blush or turn red. Another person might break out in a cold sweat and suddenly feel chilled. All of these physiological changes indicate that EFT is working.

- **The person feels vibrating energy.** Do enough tapping and your fingers will begin to tingle. When that happens, move your open hands toward each other, moving them closer, further apart, and closer again. If you sense a vibrating energy field or a feeling of resistance that grows stronger as your hands move closer, something is happening energetically.

- **A cognitive shift occurs.** One minute you're angry and the next you're laughing. One minute the person you're mad at can't do anything right and the next you're making excuses for him. One minute you're convinced that there is only one way, one "right" and "true" way, to look at the situation and the next you realize there are many. As soon as you stop replaying a situation in the same old way and notice something new or different, and as soon as "the principle of the thing" no longer matters the way it did, it's obvious that EFT has done its job.

- **The pain moves.** In EFT sessions that involve physical pain, this happens so often that we use the phrase "chasing the pain" to describe the appropriate EFT response. The pain might move a short distance, such as an inch or two, but it's often a longer distance, such as from the left eye to the right side of the forehead or from the right shoulder blade to the center of the spine. In some cases, pain jumps all over the body. The pain changing locations is a sign that EFT is producing a shift.

- **The pain gets worse.** Ironically, this can be a sign that EFT is working. It often indicates that buried emotional issues are getting close to the surface. By continuing to tap and by approaching the pain and its aspects from a different perspective, your results will probably improve. It's very unusual for pain to get worse and stay worse when you're using EFT, especially when you incorporate the shortcuts and advanced techniques explained in this book.

- **The person is suddenly open to new options.** This is an excellent sign because it shows that the person is no longer stuck in his or her old way of thinking and feeling. A balanced emotional state leads to clear thinking.

The overall test is whether *any* kind of change is taking place. The more things change, the more EFT is working. Even if you haven't yet achieved the results you hope for, all this movement is a very good sign. It's only when nothing happens—the pain stays exactly where it was, the person's attitude doesn't shift at all, and the whole situation stays stuck—that we are tempted to conclude that EFT was not effective.

When that happens, it's worth tapping more. Sometimes that's all it takes. At other times, identifying core issues and previously overlooked aspects can turn an unresponsive situation into an EFT success story. I've seen this so many times that I never conclude that EFT "didn't work." Rather, I adopt the belief that EFT always works, but that sometimes we have to keep searching for the problem's true emotional cause.

The next chapter will add to the EFT skills you've already learned and enhance your ability to achieve good results for you and everyone you'd like to help.

Terrorist Attacks and
Other Nightmares

Civilian populations are affected by natural and man-made disasters even more than military populations are. Unlike military personnel, police, and rescue workers, most people haven't received any training or experience that would help them anticipate or cope with the aftermath of terrible events. Fortunately, EFT tapping can fill that void. Here is how some EFT practitioners helped themselves and others deal with the unexpected.

One week after the 2001 attacks on the World Trade Center in New York City, Dr. Carol Look, whose office is two miles away, shared the following suggestions for traumatized therapists and details about the escape of a traumatized client. Throughout her report, you will find helpful insights and language to use in tapping for yourself and others.

EFT and the Aftermath of 9/11

by Dr. Carol Look

Many of the survivors who worked until last week in the World Trade Center have been experiencing the classic cluster of symptoms of post-traumatic stress disorder, including auditory and visual flashbacks, an exaggerated startle response, nightmares, profound restlessness, and a heightened state of agitation. I would like to address the population of people experiencing a milder, scaled down version of PTSD. While their symptoms are less severe than those of people who barely escaped with their lives, they are still unbearable and deserve and require competent treatment.

Some of those New Yorkers who did not lose family members are experiencing deep grief as a result of being glued to the news accounts of the tragedy and from seeing hundreds of photograph posters of the missing that make the loss of complete strangers all the more personal. They are also grieving the symbol of downtown, the buildings that represented the commerce of the country. They can't get away from the constant sound of sirens, day and night, the smell of smoke and destruction, and the look of terror on neighbors' faces. Friends and clients are unsettled in the present, afraid of the future, and "unhinged" by last week's attack.

The most prevalent emotional symptoms for people suffering in this second tier of PTSD include feelings of guilt, helplessness, and anxiety. In addition, I have observed signs of distraction (people staring at you but not hearing what you are saying), emotional numbness (shock), mild disorientation (getting into the shower with socks or glasses on), irritability (picking fights with loved ones), losing orientation to time and space (missing important meetings/bumping into things), and being dissociated from feelings and events. Strong feelings of "survivor's guilt" are preventing individuals from validating or expressing their feelings, and a strong sense of feeling unsafe is preventing people from making wise, centered decisions in their daily lives. These emotional states and their oppressive consequences can be efficiently handled with EFT.

Suggestions for a Traumatized Therapist

It is not just weekly clients who feel disoriented, exhausted, frustrated, and traumatized. Therapists are, of course, among those New Yorkers who need help. Hundreds of mental health workers have lost patients and loved ones or witnessed the devastation directly, yet they expect themselves to be ready and emotionally available to comfort others. Numerous colleagues have been telling me that they feel they went back to work too early.

Many described feeling stunned and unprepared for hearing the horror stories and fears of their clients, one after another, all day long. One social worker said she was overwhelmed by her patients' actual experiences. Several of her clients had waited until feeling surrounded by the safety of their therapist's office to tell every last detail of the catastrophe.

Still other colleagues said they were under the impression that they were coping well and processing what had happened until stories of unprecedented devastation were recounted in their offices. Colleagues are telling me they are going to work without their appointment books, double-booking their sessions, making poor logistical decisions, failing to carry out routine chores, and feeling empty, lonely, helpless, and afraid. One therapist told me she felt useless as a professional and was "leaking" her own emotions all over the place.

As mental health professionals, we must be able to take care of ourselves in order to offer comfort and care to others. When I volunteered at the Armory for the families who were directed there to report missing loved ones, numerous mental health workers appeared nearly as traumatized and disoriented as the family members. Some social workers were so eager to "help" that they were emotionally intrusive and missed important clues from the distressed families.

Some of the most effective EFT practitioners I know "forgot" to seek help or treat themselves and only compounded their feelings of distress by volunteering too long or going back to work too soon. A seasoned clinician told me he feared he had added to the emotional damage of his clients by being too distraught himself to be present.

Here are some useful Setup Phrases for overwhelmed therapists:

Even though I don't want to hear about it anymore...

Even though my clients' fears scare me...and I feel overwhelmed...

Even though I shouldn't want to protect myself from the stories...

Even though I should be doing more...helping more (I am enough...I do enough)...

Even though I resent their neediness when I have my own needs...

Even though I'm mad at her for telling me the gruesome details (I wish I hadn't heard that story)...

Even though I want to be taken care of instead of taking care of them...

Even though I feel guilty...I should be able to handle this...

Even though I'm afraid of the hatred I'm hearing about...I choose love...

Even though I wasn't afraid of the future until they reminded me to be...

Even though I feel helpless and powerless...I want to feel safe...

Even though I can't stop seeing the images in my head...

Treatment for a Client Who Escaped

I wanted to share a portion of the treatment process I used with a client who felt guilty and unsafe as a result of last week's devastation.

This morning I worked with Jen who had been attending a meeting in a building directly across the street from the World Trade Center when the attack occurred. She escaped through a southern entrance of the building, was covered in soot, and crawled under a fence with other employees to safety at the tip of the island. Jen has a sketchy memory of the morning, and she told me she was in "survivor mode" all day, blocking her feelings of fear and vulnerability. It was quite evident she had been traumatized.

First we tapped for:

Even though I still feel jittery, and scared of the future…

Even though I don't feel safe in New York anymore…

Even though I can't believe I went through that incident…

Even though I feel threatened…I can and do take care of myself…

At various treatment spots, I alternated *"I feel safe now"* with *"I'm not safe"* until Jen calmed down. (Please note that using the Tell the Story Technique is also very helpful. The clients are already tuned in and just narrate what happened — *"and then…and then…and then…"* — while they tap on themselves or you tap on them.)

We then turned to Jen's feelings of guilt. She described herself as "fine" and not nearly as traumatized as other people who lost their loved ones. She felt guilty about receiving attention and help. She said she felt overwhelmed by the enormity of the problem, even aware that I, her therapist, must be going through trauma. Jen also felt wracked with guilt because she had burst into hysterical giggles and laughter Friday evening. She felt totally out of balance, although she enjoyed and needed the release. With EFT, Jen was able to reframe her outburst as a natural release of intense emotion, rather than humor that she feared offended others.

Even though I shouldn't have been laughing...

Even though I feel guilty for being upset...when I wasn't hurt as much as others...

Even though I shouldn't get the attention...others deserve it more than I...

Even though I feel guilty getting on with my life...I choose to take care of my needs...

Even though I feel guilty for not doing more...for wanting to change the subject...

These rounds produced a deeper awareness of guilt and physical feelings in her chest and throat that needed attention.

Even though I have this heaviness in my chest...the dust and the screams...

Even though I have this anxiety in my throat...I'm afraid to stay in New York...

Even though the future is so uncertain...and I'm afraid of what is going to happen...

Even though I'm afraid I'm in denial... (People kept telling her she was in denial and would fall apart in the near future.)

Jen described feeling deeply conflicted between two sets of experiences and feelings:

1.   Feelings of shock and terror when in her downtown home, where she compulsively watched the news around the clock, and

2.   Feelings of relief she felt when working uptown in Manhattan where she found people seemingly oblivious to it all—with an absence of reminders such as candlelight vigils or hospitals teeming with families and people in crisis. She wasn't sure which emotional state was "right" or appropriate.

Even though I don't know where I fit in…nothing feels stable anymore…

Even though I feel guilty for wanting to run away…

Even though I don't want to burden other people with my fears…

Even though I don't know how to react, I choose to love and accept myself anyway.

Even though I need a break from it all, I accept all of me.

We kept tapping until Jen regained the confidence in her own ability to handle what she had experienced.

❀ ❀ ❀

In the next report, Rebecca Marina offers a firsthand account of a successful EFT treatment for the trauma experienced by a hurricane survivor.

EFT for a Hurricane Katrina Survivor

by Rebecca Marina

It is important to preframe this story by telling you that Paulette is a very gifted intuitive healer and medium. She knew something was coming to New Orleans, but she refused to "see." She felt devastated that she was no longer in a position to help others because of her own extreme emotional trauma.

Paulette lived only five blocks from the Mighty Mississippi in downtown New Orleans. She heard Katrina was coming and, like so many others, fled reluctantly. She took only the bare minimum, thinking she would be back in 2 or 3 days. Here is her story.

At the beginning of our phone session, Paulette was almost hysterical and exhausted from her ordeal. She felt hopeless, abandoned, betrayed, and very angry at people for criticizing the officials in New Orleans. Worse, she doubted that she could ever do her work again. She felt as if she had absolutely nothing left in this world.

I asked Paulette to tell me a little of her story, so we could address her most pressing emotions first. Paulette could hardly talk. She rated her level of anxiety and confusion at a 10 and reported feeling foggy, numb, hopeless, disconnected, displaced, and angry.

We began by addressing her feelings of being displaced, confused, and foggy headed:

> *Even though I feel so confused, my life is upside down, and I don't know what to do…*

Even though I don't understand why this had to happen to me...

Even though I don't understand why this sneaked up on me, I refused to "see" this coming...

I release this fear that has gotten hold of me...

I've always been the strong one, it's hard for me to ask for help...

I can't help anyone else now and I don't know what to do...

I am afraid I won't be able to help anyone and I won't be able to do my work...

When we rechecked Paulette's intensity on "confusion," she felt it was a 6. I should have asked how she knew it was a 6 because Paulette became distracted and started talking about how angry she felt that the media were criticizing the mayor of New Orleans so much.

She started to get very emotional and I had Paulette tap on herself while telling me the story. Tell the Story is a wonderful technique for dissolving emotions. Just tap while talking about the situation or event that bothers you.

When Paulette was a bit calmer, I told her we would "harness the power" of her anger. I explained that anger, used properly, can help transform negative to positive in very short order.

I asked Paulette to give me some details of why she felt angry, and we had some great Setup Statements in:

Even though I feel so angry at the media for criticizing the mayor—at least he didn't leave—I love and accept myself.

Even though I feel so angry at the Red Cross and the Salvation Army for selling clothes, buy one get one free, I love and accept myself.

Even though I feel so angry I could just scream [and she did scream a few choice words], *I deeply love and accept myself.*

We then stopped and Paulette said she now felt great! I asked her to recheck the original emotion of confusion and it was down to none at all.

We then tapped in some positive choices using Dr Carrington's Choices phrasing (see chapter 8). Paulette became more calm, centered, and ready to pick up the pieces and move forward. The difference was incredible.

✻ ✻ ✻

In the following account, certified EFT Universe practitioner Karen Degen from Christchurch, New Zealand, shares how EFT alleviated the PTSD many people suffered after a string of severe earthquakes there. In the case of Karen's client "Lee," it took just two sessions.

EFT Resolves Earthquake PTSD in 2 Sessions
by Karen Degen, EFT INT-1

In Christchurch, New Zealand, we experienced a series of extremely damaging earthquakes, beginning in

September 2010. Many people experienced posttraumatic stress disorder (PTSD) from these earthquakes, especially the one in February 2011 where most of the city was destroyed. Those who were in the city that day and experienced the collapsing buildings and the death and destruction around them were the worst affected.

One of those people was Lee, who came to me more than a year later in June 2012. She was feeling very anxious and unhappy and suffering from migraines. Any time there was a loud noise or if the phone rang, she would scream. Although the people at work understood, as they had been through the same thing, it was still very hard for everyone to deal with. Because there were so many people screaming during and after the earthquake, her current screaming was also retraumatizing her workmates. She had been receiving the free counseling that the government provided for all citizens of Christchurch after the earthquakes, but it was not working for her.

During our first EFT session, we primarily used the Movie Technique to deal with the memories of seeing the destruction and the people who were broken and dying. We also tapped separately on the aspects of guilt, fear, and feeling the violent shaking.

At our second session, Lee reported that she had only screamed twice in the intervening week and felt a lot better. We tapped some more on the feeling of the ground moving beneath her feet and also the fear of not knowing what to do. At this point, testing showed that her trauma was gone. We had a couple more sessions to deal with other things that seemed to be affecting her happiness, then a few months later I received this lovely e-mail from her:

I hope you are well! I've been meaning to e-mail you for weeks and tell you my news. I'm now 23 weeks' pregnant! The IVF worked the first time, which was incredible. We have found out that it's a girl and I'm very excited to meet her in 4 months.

I really want to thank you because when I think back to this time last year when I had posttraumatic stress disorder, I was so unhappy. I know that my body and mind were in no shape to carry a child. I know that some people take years to get over PTSD (if ever!) and I felt back to normal after two sessions with you! I don't think I would be having a baby in 17 weeks if it weren't for you and EFT. Thank you so much!

* * *

In the following report, EFT practitioner Lori Lorenz gives us the details of an intense case of trauma. This is an example of a case that should only be handled by professionals. Experienced healing practitioners have all had cases where clients protected themselves by repressing or "not remembering" childhood events that involve torture, maiming, murder, sexual abuse, and other unspeakable atrocities. Sometimes these clients appear to lead a normal life until these memories show up and cause severe disorientation.

Lori refers in passing to a "forest" of problems. This is a reference to the analogy used in EFT that when you cut down a few trees in a forest of traumatic memories, often the whole forest collapses, making it unnecessary to address each of the other trees individually.

For privacy reasons, the actual atrocities are not described and, as with most of the reports in this book, the client's name has been changed.

Where Only the Pros Should Tread

by Lori Lorenz

Trish was referred to me by a caring family member because, despite her outwardly beautiful, active, loving family life, she seemed to be falling apart. Within the past few weeks, terrifying dreams and intrusive waking images from her childhood began appearing out of "nowhere." Even though she knew her childhood was not pleasant and that her family was pretty dysfunctional, these "memories" were outside the realm of anything she thought could actually occur in *any* family, least of all hers. She was terrified of both the "memories" (if they were true) and the possibility that she was "going insane" (if they weren't).

When Trish entered my office, she was barely holding herself together. Within minutes, she was relating the extreme content of these new memories and entering into gripping states of flashback and immobilizing terror, eyes glazed and unfocused, body shaking.

Even with an established relationship and familiarity with the client's history, most practitioners find such a situation to be pretty unnerving. In the "old days," there was little one could do during this ordeal but provide comfort, keep the person oriented, and introduce some countering thoughts. With our EFT tools, however, we have much more with which to help.

Using a strong voice, I kept reminding Trish where she was and asking her to keep looking into my eyes to help her orient herself. It seemed that a strong and directive voice was needed to help her focus as she moved in and out of being present. I briefly explained EFT as this "weird stuff" of tapping on the meridians to process the emotions and, despite her strong skepticism, she was willing to try, even though she was quite sure nothing could help her.

In EFT, I often use the TAB (Touch and Breathe) method (see chapter 6), which can be very soothing and introspective. Instead of tapping, you simply hold each acupoint while breathing in and breathing out. But in this case, strong tapping seemed the best way to get her body sensations going in order to counter the body memories and the feeling of being disconnected from her body that seemed to be overwhelming her. So we started tapping on *"this emotion," "this terror,"* and *"this overwhelm."* At times I had to tap and speak for her when she was immobilized, which I did with her permission. After several rounds of EFT tapping, she was able to achieve some orientation and a sense of calm. I'll never forget the look of disbelief on her face when she sat back, looked at me with clearly present eyes, and said she couldn't believe it, but whatever this stuff was, it was working.

As Trish calmed somewhat, she expressed her greater fear that she was going crazy, that these memories couldn't be true, and that people just didn't do these things to children. I let her know that, unfortunately, people do, but we didn't have to decide anything about the truth of her images at that point, we just wanted her out of this terror and sense of feeling overwhelmed.

So we started the Tearless Trauma Technique by simply referring to *"these memories," "these images," "this terror,"* and *"this confusion"* while I reminded her frequently not to go into the memories in detail. She was intentionally to distance herself from them, without dissociating, and just guess at what she might feel if she were to touch into them. I kept reminding her that our intent was not to go into the experience yet, and this helped her discover that she had some control over the intrusiveness of the thoughts as well as the feeling of being overwhelmed.

Once Trish had a sense that she could use EFT to counter the intensity of the memories, she began to describe them. We worked carefully with the details and tapped often whenever the intensity rose. There was little hope of coming down to 0 on any of these far-reaching, many-aspected events, and there was little time to keep track of these 0-to-10 measurements anyway. Nonetheless, we did some general monitoring of the intensity and her sense of whether or not she could handle it. For Trish, at least at that moment, having a place to describe these horrific events seemed more important for her sense of sanity than trying to neutralize a "forest" of unknown extent in a single two-hour session.

By the end of our first session, Trish was absolutely convinced of the efficacy of EFT. She was determined to use it as much as was needed to take back her ability to live her own life while working through whatever was needed to discover the truth and heal it. By our meeting the next day, she had used EFT extensively for the memories and nightmares, with impressive relief.

In the past 8 months, Trish has discovered the truth of these memories, received several validations from external sources, and has courageously faced layer after layer of experience that would not be believed by most people—even in a horror film or documentary. Her experience of calculated abuse over more than a decade ranks among the most intense I've encountered or read about. And that's saying a lot because my work has included the type of intense trauma that has resulted in multiple personality disorder and severely repressed memories. Through this healing, in which her primary tool has been EFT, Trish has grown and deepened in her capacity to love, experience joy, and connect with her husband and children in ways that amaze her and bring tears to her eyes.

The fact that she has reached this point in only 8 months is almost unheard of, even for less extensive mind-controlling abuse than she suffered. At one point in our work, Trish considered having a local therapist work with her in person. I travel to her city only every 4 to 6 weeks, and we work by phone between trips.

Trish interviewed five or six professionals who specialize in abuse, each of whom either gave a dismal prognosis and predicted years of painful, traumatizing work to get through the experiences she outlined or simply declined to work with her. Wisely, Trish opted to stay with EFT. She occasionally schedules a session or two when some new aspect or layer of experience surfaces. The rest she handles with EFT using her (by now) excellent skills, and those issues are getting easier to clear, with faster results.

❀ ❀ ❀

EFT for Combat PTSD

There are many accounts by combat veterans of how EFT helped resolve their PTSD. In the following article, Evan Hessel, former president of the Viking Vets, who served in Iraq, Nov 2006–Feb 2008, and Afghanistan, May 2009–June 2010, tells how he used EFT to free himself from PTSD when nothing else had produced lasting results.

A Vet Tells His Story

by Evan Hessel

EFT worked for me, and it can work for you.

I lost 11 brothers on my first deployment alone. Their initials are tattooed on the inside of my left forearm in memorial. I will never forget them. But I will not let their loss cripple me emotionally for life, either.

If you are at all like me, your first thought—if you are even aware of EFT to begin with—is that this stuff is a bunch of BS. How the hell can tapping on your face and hands alleviate PTSD? But I was wrong, and found this program to be far more effective—and less emotionally invasive—than anything else I have tried for combatting PTSD.

When I got out of the army and moved back to Oregon in late 2010, I planned to take some time to clear my head. I wanted to avoid responsibility, and I sure as hell didn't want anyone telling me what to do. I was glad to be free of the overly structured military life.

Six months later, I could barely leave the house. Nearly all of my personal relationships were strained—or worse. And I had almost zero interest in anything but wallowing in my own self-pity. At the urging of my family, I finally sought treatment at the VA in the spring of 2011.

I started a 6-month traditional PTSD therapy program at the Vancouver outpatient clinic (part of the Portland VA Medical Center system). To track my progress, my therapist had me complete a PTSD Checklist–Military (PCL-M) at the start of every other session.

The PCL-M asks the veteran to rate the severity and/or prevalence of 17 different PTSD symptoms on a scale from 1 (Not at all) to 5 (Extremely). Answering "not at all" to each question would produce a final score of 17, while answering "extremely" to each question would produce a final score of 85. A score of 50 or higher is the field's accepted cutoff for a veteran having PTSD.

My first PCL-M score was in the mid 70s. When I finished the VA program in the fall of 2011, I was in the low 40s, below the threshold. Outstanding improvement to be sure, but it didn't stick. Within a few months, many of the symptoms had returned.

My emotional condition continued to deteriorate throughout 2012. I had dismissed Viking Vets e-mails about the Emotional Freedom Techniques for months, immediately deleting each without even a cursory glance. Around Thanksgiving 2012, I finally relented—again at the urging of my family—and set up an appointment. I decided to complete a six-session (one per week, or more spaced out if you prefer) treatment program.

My EFT provider, like the VA, had me complete a PCL-M prior to the first session, after the third and sixth (final) sessions, as well as 90 and 180 days after completing the program. Here is how I looked:

Before session 1: 54. While not considered extreme PTSD, it is certainly above the cutoff.

After session 3: 35. This was only 2 weeks after the first session.

After session 6: 27. This was half the score of when I started the program, but the progress is even more substantial considering my final score was only 10 points above the rock-bottom minimum one can score on the PCL-M.

90-day follow-up: 32

180-day follow-up: 32 (no change!). I have not had a single nightmare or involuntary reaction (i.e., jumping at a loud noise or breathing hard when remembering a stressful experience downrange, etc.) in almost a year. While I will always remember the men who died and the moments when they did, my emotions no longer control me.

The Veterans Stress Project offers no-cost EFT to veterans, and testimonials and symptom improvement information from veterans who have utilized the program. If you would rather not meet with an EFT provider in person, they can also conduct sessions via Skype. Or, if you'd rather not interact with a provider at all, there are videos on the Internet that can guide you through a session.

A simple search of YouTube for "Battletap" produces these and several others, for emotions such as stress, shame, insomnia, and fear. I strongly recommend trying one for yourself. If you feel like a video has helped, even a little, I further encourage you to visit www.battletap.org, where you can create a personal account and complete customized sessions.

What do you have to lose? Give it a shot!

* * *

Here is another story by a veteran. Olli found relief through EFT from the dissociated state he had been living in since his return from deployment in Iraq and the many horrors he experienced there.

From a Downward to an Upward Spiral

by Olli

I deployed with 10th Mountain Division, 2nd BCT, to Baghdad from September 2006 through June 2007. I performed a variety of jobs including guard, medical lab, medic, and pharmacy work. My experience was a typical mosaic of long days, stress, and a variety of emotionally powerful events.

In short, I was exposed to the following experiences (some face-to-face and others indirectly through my comrades): IED explosions, small arms fire, rocket attacks, sniper attacks, wounded and dead Americans, allies, and Iraqis (military, enemy, and civilians—including women and children), mass casualty, suicide, self-mutilation, divorce, infidelity, fist fights, rape, captured and beheaded U.S. soldiers, imprisoned terrorists, smell and sights of bloody, decomposing, and burnt tissues, booby traps, destroyed vehicles, and a persistent fear of being attacked.

Upon my return from deployment, I began my first year of medical school. Even though I completed the first academic year with good grades, I noticed that my quality of life had diminished significantly. I recognized that I was no longer able to be present in the moment and was always observing whatever was happening in my life from a "witness" perspective.

I also replayed many situations in my mind, often thinking of how I could have done them differently. I no longer laughed much and felt burdened by my past, reminiscing my days when ignorance was bliss.

A year went by and I had spoken about my experiences to a variety of people in attempts to "release" them or find peace from their recurrent nature. Talking about the experiences helped me a bit, but only on an intellectual level. I understood that what I was feeling was "a normal reaction to an abnormal situation."

I knew that I had done my best and was a force of good in this world. But I also knew that my symptoms persisted even after talking about them. Otherwise I was doing "fine" and identified my symptoms as recurring emotions that were independent of my intellect. They were in a way unreachable, no matter how I tried to resolve or release them. I concluded that this was the price I had to pay, and continued to live my unrewarding life to the best of my ability.

About a month ago I had a powerful experience. I met an old acquaintance who knew me before I deployed to Iraq. Nancy asked if I was open to letting her try something called EFT to help me gain freedom from my recurring emotions. She said it was an "emotional" tool and not a mental one. I agreed and we spent a total of 4 hours doing the work over 2 days.

The results were immediate and I literally "fell back" into my body from a defensive posture that I had unknowingly created in my mind. I could feel my body again and could not stop crying and laughing. I could now be present in the moment and not have half of my attention observing the situation as it was happening.

I also became less reactive to whistle sounds and sirens that used to initiate in me a fight-or-flight response, as incoming rockets had done in Iraq. Overall, I regained the quality of life that I had prior to deployment.

It was truly an "emotional freedom" technique. Since then, I have been on a constant upward spiral and have been able to transform my past into a great strength. We worked through every single memory and emotion that I was not at peace with and "tapped them out." I also learned how to "self-administer" EFT and have been practicing it on myself whenever something new has emerged from my past.

* * *

Rather than the downward spiral that so many veterans with PTSD fall into, one that ends in alcoholism, domestic violence, hospitalization, joblessness, or even homelessness, this veteran has now gone on to become a psychiatrist. He has been instrumental in getting EFT to many other veterans suffering from PTSD.

Many therapists have discovered the same effects when they use EFT. The following account is an open letter by clinical psychologist Constance Louie-Handelman, PhD, a former captain in the U.S. Army Reserve, who was in charge of a forward operating base in Kandahar Province in Afghanistan. She writes how, after just one round of EFT tapping, soldiers were noticeably more relieved and calmer.

How EFT Helps Active-Duty Warriors

by Constance Louie-Handelman, PhD, Captain, USAR

I began investigating Emotional Freedom Techniques (EFT) when a friend told me about tapping. Although I have a PhD degree in clinical psychology, I was continually searching for other effective techniques that could help clients. I studied EMDR, neuro-linguistic programming (NLP), and hypnotherapy.

However, after studying and practicing EFT, I found it worked quickly in eliminating fears, limiting beliefs, and pain, and releasing traumatic events. Every opportunity I had, I used EFT with family, friends, and clients and achieved excellent long-lasting results. I was so confident in EFT that I felt I had something to offer when I read about the high rate of suicide among U.S. soldiers.

I was commissioned as a captain in the U.S. Army Reserve on March 2010, and was deployed to Afghanistan from July 2011 to May 2012. As a psychologist, I was in charge of a forward operating base in Kandahar Province and officially saw 199 individual soldiers (574 sessions).

Once I established rapport, understood their problems and needs, I used EFT primarily for anger, sleep, depression, and stress.

After just one round of tapping, soldiers were noticeably more relieved and calmer. Soon thereafter, soldiers added more details about their problems, or expressed issues that they had kept to themselves for years. When they felt the profound positive result, it was then easy to encourage soldiers to learn how to tap, something they could do themselves in a matter of minutes, in order to release past, current, or anticipated problems, or "preemptive tapping," as one soldier called it.

The ease to learn and to apply the tapping was an important element of EFT since I often saw a solider just for one session.

I realized the success of EFT when soldiers were able to return to full duty, wanting to learn more about EFT, or referring other soldiers to my office. Since returning home, I am disheartened to learn that EFT is not an accepted technique in the U.S. Department of Veterans Affairs (VA). Fortunately, there is the Veterans Stress Project (www.stressproject.org) that offers free EFT sessions for returning vets.

I can only hope that the VA's powers-that-be will soon realize the effectiveness of EFT in order to help thousands of suffering vets, thus making a dramatic dent in the suicide rate.

❊ ❊ ❊

Although Dr. Louie-Handelman's wish for the VA to recognize the effectiveness of EFT hasn't come true yet, progress has been made. When she returned from deployment, she was hired by the San Francisco Veterans Center where she now offers EFT to veterans.

In the following article, Lindsay Kenny shares details of her work with veterans during a week in San Francisco, California, in 2008. She was part of a team of EFT practitioners who worked with volunteer veterans diagnosed with PTSD as a result of experiences associated with war in Vietnam, Iraq, or Afghanistan. Their EFT sessions and follow-up are documented in the film *Operation: Emotional Freedom*, produced by Eric Huurre.

The insights Lindsay offers here into commonalities in the disorder and how to approach PTSD are beneficial for counselors and practitioners who work with this population. The method she describes is highly effective for complex and challenging cases. It also provides a sense of safety that is vital for clients with PTSD.

Providing that safety helps establish rapport between client and practitioner. Lindsay notes that the gentleness of the approach makes it a good choice for those who want to try EFT on their own.

Tapping for Collections of Traumas

by Lindsay Kenny

During the week of working with combat veterans in San Francisco, I was struck by childhood issues that the veterans shared. I worked with nine of the 11 participants and I don't think there was a single one who didn't have significant baggage from childhood. It occurred to me that they were attracted to military service because it gave structure to their lives. A lot of them had repressive, domineering, dictatorial, judgmental, critical parents, which is interesting when you consider the behavior of most drill sergeants and commanding officers.

The veterans who have the most difficult time, I think, are those who experience terrible things all their lives, in childhood, during the war, and after they come home. Unhappy events get layered on top of each other until the person reaches a breaking point. I call this "piling on." When someone goes on a shooting spree or has a total breakdown, it's never because of a single event. It's one thing after another until it's like the straw that breaks the camel's back, and the person just snaps.

In the first session with each of the nine veterans I worked with in San Francisco, I started with the long-ago past. Each of the participants had completed a personal history and, in preparation for the EFT sessions, we read about events in their lives that were shocking. Rather than focusing on recent events, I started each session by asking the person about things that happened in childhood, the first traumas that he or she experienced. This was an effective way to introduce EFT, and it also established rapport.

The participants could see that EFT worked, that it could help them get over some serious issues painlessly and that they could trust us. It was also a sensible place to start because a lot of them weren't ready to talk about their war experiences. It was a way of establishing a foundation or background, which is what I do whenever I'm teaching EFT. Start with your childhood, start with the very old traumas, and then you can sneak up on current problems.

The veterans dealt with their most serious traumas in different ways. Some just stated what happened, like "I had to watch my best friend get blown up and then I had to pick up his arms and legs and put them in a body bag," as if they were reading a phone number. In those cases, I started right in on the event's different aspects and their intensity; the sights, smells, and sounds; and finally, the actual events themselves. Once the remembered sights, smells, and sounds generated less intensity, that's when I dealt with their emotions: the grief, anger, betrayal, frustration, and that sort of thing.

In PTSD counseling, if the person can talk about a trauma and name it, that's an effective way to proceed.

That's very different from the approach you have to take with people who don't want to talk about what happened. They may say, "I'm afraid to bring it up, I've got it buried, I don't want to think about it."

In EFT, we have gentle ways of sneaking up on problems, such as the Tearless Trauma Technique (see chapter 6). You don't have to describe the details of a specific problem to get good results. You can give it a title like "That Summer Night" or "The Afternoon in Baghdad," and that's all you have to say. You can tap to defuse the emotion and gradually peel away the layers before you ever get to the specifics.

For most of the veterans, the problem wasn't one single event, it was a series of events, several different things. I like to collect these before we begin, by bundling together a series of negative repetitive events that are similar or related, which in this case included things like bombs going off, sounds of gunfire, people disappearing, watching people die, seeing collections of body parts, and other horrific things.

I would say, "Just imagine, without thinking of any specific events, all those times that you were traumatized during the war, hearing gunfire at night, hearing bombs go off, and having friends not come back. Put all of those events together without focusing on any one of them, just put them in a bundle and give the bundle a name, like 'Horrific War Trauma' or 'My Nightmare in Afghanistan.' Now, if you allowed yourself to get upset, but don't go there, what do you guess your level of intensity would be on a scale from 0 to 10?"

It was always a 10, or some would say, "It's a 20." Then we would tap that whole collective bundle of trauma down to a low number, at which point the person would often say something like, "You know, what really bothers me is the time I found my friend's finger with his college ring on it," or some specific memory that really bothered him or her. We would then move from the general to the specific while the person remained relaxed and comfortable.

One huge thing that stood out to me, which they all experienced in the service, was a horrific sense of betrayal. They all felt betrayed by a superior officer, by their branch of the service, by their country, or by someone or something. This got layered onto whatever other betrayals they had already experienced in life.

The anger that they held onto often kept a trauma alive. They wanted to keep that anger and that sense of betrayal in order to keep alive thoughts about punishing whoever or whatever they were mad at. That's like drinking poison and hoping the person you're mad at gets sick or dies. But it was very hard for them to imagine any other way of responding until we tapped on the issue. Then, in most cases, the sense of betrayal and all the emotional intensity that went with it disappeared in a single session.

Each session lasted an hour and 15 minutes, and often we would deal with more than one issue during a session. Everyone had problems with stress, anxiety, insomnia, night sweats, night terrors, TMJ (temporomandibular joint problems) from clenching the jaw, or tinnitus, which is a ringing in the ears. Not all of them had seen actual combat. One participant got PTSD just from being in the service but not in a war, complete with anxiety, night sweats, paranoia, insomnia, TMJ, and pain. Others had PTSD from having family members in the service.

Every morning, we reviewed the participants' progress by going over the list of what we had worked on the day before or in previous sessions. I asked general questions like, "How are you doing with insomnia? Were you able to sleep last night?" The usual reply was "I got a great night's sleep, the best sleep I've had in 30 years." Then we'd go to the next item on the list, like TMJ or tension in the neck, checking on each physical symptom and making note of its improvement.

Of the nine vets I worked with in San Francisco using this method, all experienced significant improvement. They went through tremendous changes in their attitudes, their outlook on life, and how they felt about themselves.

I worked with one woman who was the mother of one of the veterans. She came in with symptoms that were very similar to her son's, and was able to quickly collapse all of them. After the first day, when she went from a 10 to a 0 on 15 to 20 separate issues, we really didn't have anything for her to do. She was in a very happy mode.

It was absolutely astonishing to see someone cringing and walking with short, uncomfortable steps while struggling down the hall, with a tense scowl on his face and anger permeating out of every cell, avoiding eye contact with everyone, then seeing the same person 2 or 3 days later striding confidently, with a smile on his face, joking with the other participants, happy, walking upright, and looking people in the eye.

When these guys first arrived, they were tense with each other and with themselves, and their attitude toward us was so hostile that we were a little afraid. By the end of the week, they all went out to dinner together and were laughing, joking, and having such a great time that they were asked to tone it down. You would never have known that this was the same group of traumatized people who had been tense, isolated, and miserable just a few days before.

To keep track of their progress, in addition to noting their test scores, I kept in e-mail contact with everyone I worked with for several weeks. I made sure they were doing okay and reminded them of things they planned to work on. A lot of them had projects they wanted to start, jobs they wanted to get, and in other ways move their lives in a new direction. Their physical symptoms were better, too, everything from TMJ and tinnitus to insomnia and arthritis pain or headaches. In fact, the symptoms weren't just better, they were gone.

Some of these people had to go back into situations that were difficult, such as with their families or their jobs, so they still had to deal with stress or anxiety. But after relieving themselves of substantial pain, trauma, and negativity, they reentered those situations with a clean slate. They weren't reacting the way they did in the past. They dealt with current problems at a much different level. They were calmer, more focused, had more clarity of thought and more confidence. Most important, they did it without spending months, years, or even decades in therapy or on medications.

One of the veterans was a woman who was taking care of two parents with Alzheimer's who were abusive and demanding of her time. When she came in, she was very stressed. In the service, she had been abused, molested, and raped twice. Her situation was really difficult. Yet now, after the tapping, the situation with her parents is much easier to deal with. It's not getting to her the way it used to. She's handling it more calmly and with confidence, and she uses EFT to dispel problems as they come up.

When dealing with any highly charged issue—past or chronic events or issues—you can eliminate subconscious resistance to change by tapping on the Karate Chop point while saying three times:

> *Even though I don't want to let go of these problems* [name the collective name or individual issue], *I want to love and accept who I am.*

By addressing and neutralizing that subconscious resistance head-on, the EFT process goes much more easily and quickly. After doing the reversal neutralization, you just go into normal EFT.

Then you can move from the distant past to the more recent past, and then move to the present. In each of these time frames, think of a general theme and all the events or memories that are connected to it and give it a name. Tap on that general theme until the intensity level falls to a more comfortable level. Then collect all the emotions you feel about those events and tap in a general way on those. I believe, based on my experience, that it's safer to deal with events first and then emotions.

Many people feel overwhelmed by a sense of having everything go wrong in life—they're in pain or don't feel well physically, they're in the middle of a divorce, they're facing a layoff at work, they're behind on the mortgage, and wherever they look, they see problems. When stressful events mount up, I have people write everything down so that all those problems are on a single piece of paper. When I ask them to give it a name, they'll say something like "My Hellish Life" or "This Nightmare" or "Being Overwhelmed." We tap on the list's title, using a Setup such as:

> *Even though I have this nightmare life and I'm feeling overwhelmed, I love and accept myself.*

Then we tap the EFT points, using the title as the Reminder Phrase: *My nightmare life, my nightmare life, my nightmare life.*

I think it's very difficult for most people to deal with complex issues like PTSD on their own even if they are experienced with EFT. It's a lot easier with the help of a trained, skilled professional who can guide them through it. That being said, there are people who will want to try EFT on their own, either by preference or necessity, and when they do, I believe it will help them to take this collective approach, to start by focusing not on individual events but on a collection of related events and to give the collection a name and tap on it until its intensity level drops. This is the opposite of what we normally do with EFT, but for the treatment of PTSD and other complex issues, this is a safe approach, and it works.

❀ ❀ ❀

EFT coach Ingrid Dinter, another member of the 2008 EFT team, spends considerable time working with veterans, and her gentle expertise provides an excellent model for counselors and practitioners who use EFT to help not only military personnel, but also police, emergency medical technicians, hospital staff, fire fighters, and all who have been trained to keep their feelings from interfering with their professional responsibilities. Ingrid combines general rather than specific Setups with constantly changing Reminder Phrases. This approach helps clients relax, feel comfortable, and eventually reveal core issues. In this comprehensive report, she takes us step by step through the EFT counseling process.

Introducing EFT to Combat Veterans

by Ingrid Dinter

Since I don't want new clients to get unnecessarily upset, I try not to ask too many war-related questions before I introduce EFT. Instead, we tap a few rounds on general issues, which helps the person relax. It is usually easier to explain EFT after the client has tried it and seen results.

I like to start with a round of tapping on feeling overwhelmed, as this is usually appropriate and shows respect for the client and his or her emotions. It can also help to take the edge off in a safe and comfortable way and set the stage for more tapping.

Even though I feel very overwhelmed right now, I allow myself to be surprisingly okay with that.

This Setup Statement usually startles people, as it feels appropriate. They begin to feel more relaxed, less apprehensive, and often even experience physical relief — and we were not specific, and it didn't hurt.

The word "surprisingly" opens us up to receiving new solutions and new feelings, even if we are not aware of them yet. Being open to positive surprises can fill us with expectations and curiosity, allowing us to consider new ways of dealing with our past, ways that we didn't even know were possible before.

Another statement that I use a lot is:

Even though I have been through more than you will ever understand, I choose to be surprisingly at peace with that.

Any way of phrasing this basic statement is appropriate, such as:

Even though I have been through more than anyone knows or can understand, I choose to be surprisingly okay with that.

After each round of tapping, in which I encourage the client to change any phrasing so it works better, the result can be greater trust and more relaxation. The client now sees that he or she is in control. With each round of EFT, I fill in the explanations and information the soldier needs in order to understand how and why we are so successful at releasing trauma in a gentle, fast, and nontraumatizing way.

The following are more sample Setups:

Even though I don't want to make a fool of myself by tapping on my head and body, I choose to allow myself to relax about it.

Even though I could quite easily get very emotional here and I don't want that, I choose to feel surprisingly safe and in control.

Even though I have been through more than anybody will ever understand, I choose to allow myself to heal in a way that works for me.

Even though I am overwhelmed by all that I have been through, and the mere thought of it is scary, I choose to feel confident that I can take it one step at a time, in a way that works for me.

If the veteran feels angry about the offer to help, which can be a side effect of PTSD, trust issues, or not completely establishing rapport, but he or she wants to give it just one shot, we might tap on:

Even though I resent the thought of even considering peace, healing, or forgiveness, and only veterans can understand why I am saying this and you just don't know what you are talking about, I allow myself to feel respected for all that I have been through, and I consider the possibility that I can find and accept healing in a way that works for me.

Even though _____, I allow myself to consider the possibility that I can feel safe enough to relax about it.

Even though _____, I consider being as relaxed as I was when I was 15.

Even though _____, I choose to find it surprisingly appropriate to find peace anyway.

A longer, more carefully "testing the waters" version could be:

Even though _____, I allow myself to consider that there is a way that allows me to be at peace with this in a way that works for me and everybody else involved.

And finally:

Even though _____, I choose to claim my power back in a way that feels safe and appropriate.

In my experience, veterans often don't like to talk and bring up memories that we could work on. They have a wall around themselves that keeps them safe and required some huge effort to build. As an EFT practitioner, I find it important to recognize and accept the wall for as long as the soldier needs it, as it gives a feeling of control and safety. At the same time, there are feelings and mindsets that many soldiers share. These may include feelings of being overwhelmed, misunderstood, or cheated:

Life isn't fair.

I am angry all the time.

My life is like never waking up from a bad dream.

People see me as a monster.

I feel like a failure.

I'm not able to keep my family or others safe.

I am not safe for others to be around.

My marriage is in trouble.

My buddy got killed and I couldn't help him.

My physical health is deteriorating.

I have pain where there shouldn't be pain.

I am injured and they told me that I will never recover.

I hate authority.

I am always on guard and never feel safe.

I don't trust anyone.

I suffer from insomnia.

I have intrusive thoughts.

And the list goes on. If it is safe and appropriate, it can be very healing to ask for a specific event that caused any of these feelings, beliefs, or physical symptoms, and let the soldier choose which one to tap on.

In my experience, when a veteran has suffered for so long from guilt, shame, and self-blame, an excuse, no matter how well intentioned, will be hard to accept. It may even increase the person's negative self-talk, that what happened was so bad that there is indeed no way ever to receive forgiveness unless we make something up. Instead, it can help to listen calmly and respectfully for the soldier's version of the situation.

Tapping on each component of it, using the Movie Technique and Tearless Trauma Technique, can release excess feelings about what happened. I often see that there was more to the story than what the soldier remembered or found important. In those details, we often find the true reason for what happened and why.

War has rules and a life of its own. Once soldiers become a part of war, they may be exposed to situations that force them to make decisions they later regret.

Here are some Setups that might help bring relief:

Even though war sucks, and so did my role in it, I can't believe what it made me do, and I feel guilty and responsible for the things that happened, I choose to allow myself to find peace with that in an appropriate way that truly works for me, the victims, and everybody else involved.

Even though it hurts to see what war has made of me and my dreams and values, and I feel ashamed about the whole thing, I choose to allow myself to find peace and forgiveness in surprising and appropriate ways.

Even though I wish this had never happened, and I can't forgive myself for what I have done, I choose to allow myself to heal from what war has made of me and find a better way to honor and support those who had to suffer through what happened.

Even though I can't imagine my life will ever be what it was before I left, I choose to open up to the possibility that there are ways to live a powerful, meaningful life in a way that truly works for me and those I care for.

Finding Meaning

Many veterans feel that they have a lesson to teach but suffer too much or don't feel comfortable enough to share their story or even consider being heard. Opening up that possibility can help them find power in their past:

Even though I believe that the guilt that I have felt for all these years will never be enough to make up for what happened or for what I did, I open up to the possibility that there might be a more powerful way of taking responsibility for what happened and transforming it into a powerful lesson of peace.

Even though I am sorry for what I did, and I could never express it, I allow myself now to realize that my plea for forgiveness might be heard, even by myself.

Then we do a round of tapping, using Reminder Phrases like:

I'm sorry for what happened. I ask for forgiveness and I allow myself to receive it.

❖ ❖ ❖

Do-It-Yourself EFT

Can someone who has experienced traumatic events safely learn EFT on his or her own? Can someone who is not a trained psychotherapist or other professional help a friend, spouse, or relative who suffers from PTSD? Is there a danger that the tapping will just open up old wounds and make them worse? Will the person suffer a painful abreaction?

If you have painful memories and PTSD symptoms and you choose to use EFT to help yourself, here are some suggestions for doing so. Remember, however, that professional help may be indicated, and you are urged to seek such help should difficult intensity arise.

Dr. Carol Look recommends focusing entirely on stress release and physical symptoms. "By starting with bodily symptoms and daily stress," she says, "you can do a lot to help yourself feel more comfortable while relieving discomfort."

In other words, work at first on general stress relief and whatever aches, pains, or other physical symptoms you have. This will give you an opportunity to try EFT, become familiar with the tapping points, get into the rhythm of tapping, and release some of your stress. This is the most important foundation you can lay for yourself.

Do this by working through EFT's Basic Recipe (see chapter 3) for at least three general problems. Do the complete procedure, tapping on all the EFT points with appropriate Reminder Phrases. For example:

Even though it's hard for me to relax, I fully and completely accept myself.

Even though my shoulder hurts, I fully and completely accept myself.

Even though I keep having this headache, I fully and completely accept myself.

Even though I have this overall feeling of stress or tension and I can feel it in my back, I fully and completely accept myself.

Does the EFT make a difference? If you feel less stressed and if your physical symptoms improve, which is what I expect will happen, you're learning to use EFT and your body is responding well.

After a day or two of the Basic Recipe for general stress and physical symptoms, which has prepared you for more advanced work, you can start using EFT to defuse or neutralize the emotional intensity you feel toward recent events. This is not the time to tackle intrusive traumatic memories. We're going to start small.

Assuming that this has been an ordinary week with nothing unusual going on, pick out three things that irritated you and focus on them. For example:

> *Even though I'm annoyed because the contractor didn't finish the repairs, I fully and completely accept myself.*

> *Even though my boss is being impossible, as usual, I fully and completely accept myself.*

> *Even though my kids make way too much noise, I fully and completely accept myself.*

Now review Dr. Patricia Carrington's Choices Method (see chapter 8) and add a "solution" statement to each of your Setups. For example:

> *Even though I have this overall stress and I can feel it in my back, I fully and completely accept myself, I forgive my back, which is doing the best it can, and I choose to surprise myself by relaxing and enjoying life while releasing all the stress in my back and letting my back feel flexible and comfortable in every way.*

> *Even though the contractor didn't finish the repairs and I'm really annoyed, I fully and completely accept myself. Even though it's impossible to get good help and there are always delays and it drives me nuts, I accept myself. Even though this repair business is noisy and messy and behind schedule and a real distraction, I completely accept myself and I choose to be surprised at how easy it is for me to switch my mind from the things that are going wrong to the things that are going right in my*

life, which is plenty. I choose to focus on the things that really matter, starting right now.

Try other general Setup Statements that deal with overall rather than specific symptoms, such as:

Even though I feel overwhelmed right now, I choose to be surprisingly okay with that.

Even though I don't want to do this tapping business, it's too weird, I choose to take it one step at a time in a way that truly works for me.

Even though I'm disappointed about what happened, I accept myself, and I'm willing to see it differently.

Even though I'm stuck in this anger and don't want to let it go, I'm open to the possibility that it would be nice to feel more peaceful about this.

I strongly recommend that anyone working alone study the examples these talented practitioners have provided and use them as a model when doing EFT. Work through the Basic Recipe several times a day for at least a week on general issues like stress, physical symptoms, and recent annoyances.

Having done that homework, your next assignment is to choose one or two unhappy events from the past, as far back as childhood, but not one that you have trouble talking about. Start with events that aren't very high on the 10-point intensity scale, a 3 or 4 at most. Write a Setup for the first event using all of the tips and hints you have been studying.

Only after you have done this homework, practiced on general issues, and then practiced being specific with issues that don't cause much discomfort should you tackle more serious memories.

Don't forget the Tearless Trauma Technique (see chapter 6). The instant you start to feel emotional intensity, step back and pause while you tap until you feel more relaxed. Whenever you feel uncomfortable, try a general Setup like:

Even though that makes me really uncomfortable, I fully and completely accept myself. Even though I don't feel comfortable thinking about that right now, I accept myself. Even though I don't want to think about those things, I accept and forgive myself and I choose to let this tapping business do its work so that my stress level comes way down and it's easy for me to remember what happened without being upset.

Don't rush, take your time, and when your intensity level falls to a 0 and you feel completely at ease, which often happens after tapping through the Basic Recipe once or twice, try moving forward again. If you still feel uncomfortable, no problem. Keep tapping while you say:

Even though I still have some of this uncomfortable feeling, I fully and completely accept myself.

Even though I still feel uneasy about this memory, I accept myself. Even though I don't feel like remembering what happened, I can step back from that event and just keep tapping until I feel relaxed. I choose to put it on the shelf for now, there's no pressure or deadline, and the important thing is that my energy is balanced, so I am okay, I'm safe, I'm at peace.

For even better results, include some of the phrases and recommendations referred to in this chapter or those that appear throughout this book. Underline or highlight the words that feel right for you and add them to your Setups whenever you do EFT. Write down words or phrases you would like to incorporate in your EFT work.

It is also helpful to record possible Setups in a notebook. For inspiration, peruse the archives of our free newsletter, available at www.EFTUniverse.com. EFT is like any other tool: the more you use it, the better it works. And the more you practice, the easier it is to create effective statements that address core issues and all of their aspects.

* * *

Pat Farrell successfully diagnosed and treated her own PTSD long after the car crash that caused her symptoms. Pat is a good example of someone who experienced a trauma and then manifested occasional PTSD symptoms without realizing why or without realizing what they meant. I suspect that a large number of us have had similar reactions. This do-it-yourself story offers important insights.

Accident Victim Resolves
Her Own PTSD 40 Years Later
by Pat Farrell

Three times over a period of about 25 years, I experienced shortness of breath, blood draining from my face, and heart palpitations so severe that I had to pull over while driving. Even though this occurred so seldom, these are typical symptoms of PTSD. Eventually, I started putting things together and realized that, at each occurrence, I was passing an accident just at the moment that a person on a gurney was being put into an ambulance. By this time, I was experienced in EFT and started looking for an explanation.

When I was 20, which was 40 years ago, I was trapped in a car for 3 hours while the rescue team tried to extract me after a horrible accident. Four of us in my little car were hit head-on by a 1959 Oldsmobile. That's similar to a tank running over an ant. I realized that during that time, in an unconscious or semiconscious state, I must have seen or heard the rescuers talking about my friend Rita.

It wasn't until about a week after the accident, when my family was sure that I would be okay, that they finally told me of Rita's death. While I felt shocked, I remember not really being surprised, and I realized that my subconscious was already aware of the tragedy.

Now, all these years later, I focused on the accident and used EFT to tap on:

Even though I have this stressful response each time I see a body being removed from a car...

Even though the emergency team's removal of Rita's body from the crash is deeply embedded in my subconscious...

Even though I feel responsible for Rita's death...

I tapped on the body points using wording like:

This reaction to bodies being put in an ambulance.

This reaction.

That can't be Rita on the stretcher.

I'm afraid they'll never get me out of the car.

I then used a round of:

I choose to release this subconscious reaction to seeing an accident.

I choose to release this reaction.

Then I did an entire round on guilt about Rita's death and the medical struggles that my friends and fellow passengers Frankie and Danny experienced over the years.

Even though the state police said it wasn't my fault, I have been holding on to this guilt for 40 years…

Even though I didn't feel that people blamed me, I have been holding on to this guilt…

Even though I didn't realize it, I have been punishing myself for all these years…

This guilt that it must have been my fault.

I choose to release this guilt.

I have done lots of work to release the guilt over the years and finally feel free of it thanks to EFT. EFT is truly the miracle drug—without being a drug. I would love to see more use of EFT for posttraumatic stress disorder.

❀ ❀ ❀

The next report, by Lisa Rogers, is a major testimony to persistence and points to the limitless possibilities in EFT.

How I Handled
My Child Abuse PTSD All by Myself

by Lisa Rogers

I am not a therapist, and I have no training in the mental health field. In fact, I barely graduated from high school. I am just an ordinary person who had an extraordinary problem. I suffered from posttraumatic stress disorder.

From age 12, I visited dozens of therapists trying to get help for my depression and anxiety. Years of counseling and prescribed drugs left me frustrated and no closer to relief. My frustration led me to use street drugs and alcohol in an effort to medicate myself.

When I found EFT, I had no idea then how much it would change my life. It seemed too good to be true. Nothing else had worked, but since this was something I could do on my own, I decided to give it a try. What did I have to lose? I tapped every day. My ritual was that I would tap every time I went to the bathroom. It was private and I knew I'd be there a few times a day!

Although there were many major issues I needed to address, I thought it would be helpful to focus on one at a time. I guess the best place to start is the beginning, with childhood sexual abuse.

When I was a child, I was severely abused—emotionally, physically, and sexually—by a family member. The sexual abuse began when I was 8 and continued for 4 years on a regular basis. When I told my mother, she didn't believe me. This left me with a lasting feeling of shame and guilt that somehow I had done something to cause this. My family treated me like a traitor. I felt like a freak. I ran away from home at 12 and lived on the streets for years. I was an intravenous drug user by 14 and pregnant with my first child at 15.

As the years went by, my life was a wreck. I felt alone and misunderstood. I thought I was a bad person. I hated myself and resented the world.

I was suicidal and desperate for help when I found EFT. I ordered the free *EFT Manual* and learned the process. I was afraid to dig too deep so, at first, I tapped on my physical feelings only.

> *Even though I feel like a deer in the headlights…*
>
> *Even though my heart is pounding out of my chest…*
>
> *Even though I feel like someone just jumped out and scared me…*
>
> *Even though I can't concentrate…*
>
> *Even though the noise hurts me…*
>
> *Even though the light hurts me…*
>
> *Even though I'm so nervous for no reason…*
>
> *Even though I'm terrified and I'm only watching TV…*
>
> *Even though I keep having these night terrors…*

After about a month of tapping every day on my outward symptoms, I could see that EFT really worked. I then felt confident and safe enough to start tapping on specific painful negative emotions.

Even though I hate myself...

Even though I'm trash...

Even though I'm worth nothing...

Even though I deserved it...

Even though I didn't deserve it...

Even though no child ever deserves it...

Even though my parents didn't love me...

Even though my parents didn't protect me...

Even though I should never have told...

Even though I should have told earlier but I was too scared...

Even though I told and it ruined my family and my life...

Even though I can't forget...

Even though these memories won't go away...

Even though it's been years and it still hurts so much...

Even though I feel shame and guilt...

Even though I feel different...

Even though a part of me still thinks it's my fault...

Even though I know it wasn't my fault...

Even though my mom didn't believe me...

Even though everyone thought I was a liar...

Even though it made me hate my body...

Even though child services knew and they didn't protect me...

Even though my mother knew and still won't admit it...

Even though I'll never be normal...

I just kept tapping on whatever came into my head. I would write things down to tap on later if I couldn't tap right then. I was determined. I tapped for another 6 months on a regular basis. I always checked my progress with the 0-to-10 scale.

I have to note that for the first few months I never tapped on specific abuse memories because they were too painful. I didn't want to relive them, so I simply tapped on my feelings surrounding the abuse as a whole. Once I got rid of the guilt and shame I had felt for so long, it was easier to address specific memories because I knew logically that it wasn't my fault. I have since learned to use the Tearless Trauma Technique, where you can imagine thinking about the problem without actually thinking about it. This is a great tool that I use often.

Within a year of finding EFT, my life completely changed. For over 5 years now I have been clean from drugs and alcohol and have not had a single panic attack. I now love my life and myself. EFT gave me the freedom to be a valuable and productive human being. My personal success with EFT inspired me to help others. I am now an EFT practitioner, helping people to overcome their issues with the Emotional Freedom Techniques.

❊ ❊ ❊

As a paramedic, the author of the following article witnessed some horrific scenes, which left him with PTSD. Among his multiple symptoms were near constant flashbacks and flash-forwards (he saw vivid disasters happening to people when none were occurring). He, too, was able to reverse his debilitating PTSD on his own, using EFT.

Paramedic Cures His Own PTSD

by Bob Patefield

Two and a half years ago, my 14-year career as a para-medic ended following a diagnosis of posttraumatic stress disorder (PTSD). I was in a real mess with nightmares, flashbacks, intrusive thoughts, and compulsive behaviors, to name a few.

As I traveled around, I would pass places where I had attended serious road accidents and other traumatic events, and they would vividly replay in my mind. I would see an accident in any situation. If someone simply crossed the road in front of me, I would see them fall and injure themselves in graphic detail. I would see my part-ner off to work in the morning and then was unable get images of her in a serious road accident out of my mind. It was a very unpleasant time.

I'm not sure how I got into this state. It seemed very gradual, although there were some very traumatic incidents in my career. The worst was the attempted murder of two young boys by their father. My colleague on that day never worked again, it was so distressing for him. I managed another 7 years. If only I had known about EFT then.

Although I got some basic counseling through my general practitioner, I was left on a very long waiting list to see a psychologist. I was desperate to find a self-help tool.

I had seen EFT demonstrated 2 years before, but I wasn't convinced, so when my partner had her long-standing fear of heights diffused very rapidly, I had to look in more detail.

I downloaded the manual and got tapping straight away. I was getting results almost immediately. I would spend an hour or so a day tapping on whatever issues came to mind, shifting here and there, tree to tree, using it to diffuse anxiety and stress in whatever situation arose. I ordered all the EFT materials and used them over the next year, practicing the techniques I learned on myself and others.

When I finally got my appointment to see the psychologist (after a two-year wait), she could find no traces of PTSD at all. She seemed very surprised that I had managed to deal with the PTSD myself, so I told her how I had gone about it. She seemed to think that EFT had somehow suppressed the traumatic feelings and they would resurface in the future. We know different, though.

EFT has helped me not only get over the PTSD, but has also helped me rid myself of tons of negative baggage and self-limiting beliefs from my childhood. I built a now growing business and set myself up as an EFT practitioner as well.

My whole family has benefited from these great techniques, and EFT has made us closer than we have ever been. I am currently offering a free group session to ambulance staff from my old service, not just for their benefit, but for the benefit of their patients, too. There are so many opportunities to use EFT in frontline emergency care that I almost miss being a paramedic! Hmm—night shifts. No, I changed my mind. I don't miss it at all.

* * *

References

Adams, A., & Davidson, K. (2011). *EFT comprehensive training resource level 1*. Santa Rosa, CA: Energy Psychology Press.

American Psychiatric Association. (1994). *Diagnostic and statistical manual of mental disorders* (4th ed.). Washington, DC: Author.

Angell, M. (2005). *The truth about the drug companies: How they deceive us and what to do about it*. New York, NY: Random House.

Bagot, R. C., Zhang, T. Y., Wen, X., Nguyen, T. T., Nguyen, H. B., Diorio, J., Wong, T. P., & Meaney, M. J. (2012). Variations in postnatal maternal care and the epigenetic regulation of metabotropic glutamate receptor 1 expression and hippocampal function in the rat. *Proceedings of the National Academy of Sciences USA, 109*(Suppl 2), 17200–17207. doi: 10.1073/pnas.1204599109

Bandler, R., & Grinder, J. (1979). *Frogs into princes: Neuro linguistic programming*. Moab, UT: Real People.

Bender, S. & Sise, M. (2007). *The energy of belief: Psychology's power tools to focus intention and release blocking beliefs*. Santa Rosa, CA: Energy Psychology Press.

Blanchard, E. B., Jones-Alexander, J., Buckley, T. C., & Forneris, C. A. (1996). Psychometric properties of the PTSD Checklist (PCL). *Behaviour Research and Therapy, 34*(8), 669–673.

Blanton, B. (2005). *Radical honesty: How to transform your life by telling the truth.* Reston, VA: Sparrowhawk.

Blanton, B. (2011). *Some new kind of trailer trash.* Reston, VA: Sparrowhawk.

Braverman, S. E. (2004). Medical acupuncture review: Safety, efficacy, and treatment practices. *Medical Acupuncture, 15*(3), 12–16.

Callahan, R. (1985). Five minute phobia cure: Dr. Callahan's treatment for fears, phobias, and self-sabotage. Blair, NE: Enterprise.

Callahan, R. (2000). *Tapping the healer within: Using Thought Field Therapy to instantly conquer your fears, anxieties, and emotional distress.* New York, NY: McGraw-Hill.

Chambless, D., & Hollon, S. D. (1998). Defining empirically supported therapies. *Journal of Consulting and Clinical Psychology, 66,* 7–18.

Cherkin, D. C., Sherman, K. J., Avins, A. L., Erro, J. H., Ichikawa, L., Barlow, W. E., . . . Deyo, R. A. (2009). A randomized trial comparing acupuncture, simulated acupuncture, and usual care for chronic low back pain. *Archives of Internal Medicine, 169*(9), 858–866. doi:10.1001/archinternmed.2009.65

Church, D. (2010). The treatment of combat trauma in veterans using EFT (Emotional Freedom Techniques): A pilot protocol. *Traumatology, 16*(1), 55–65. http://dx.doi.org/10.1177/1534765609347549

Church, D. (2012). The dark side of neural plasticity. *Energy Psychology: Theory, Research, and Treatment, 4*(2), 11–14.

Church, D. (2013). *The EFT manual* (3rd ed.). Santa Rosa, CA: Energy Psychology Press.

Church, D. (2014). Pain, depression, and anxiety after PTSD symptom remediation in veterans. *Explore: The Journal of Science and Healing, 10*(3), 162–169.

Church, D., & Brooks, A. J. (2010). The effect of a brief EFT (Emotional Freedom Techniques) self-intervention on anxiety, depression, pain and cravings in healthcare workers. *Integrative Medicine: A Clinician's Journal, 9*(4), 40–44.

Church, D., & Brooks, A. J. (2014). CAM and energy psychology techniques remediate PTSD symptoms in veterans and spouses. *Explore: The Journal of Science and Healing, 10*(1), 24–33.

Church, D., Geronilla, L., & Dinter, I. (2009). Psychological symptom change in veterans after six sessions of EFT (Emotional Freedom Techniques): An observational study. *International Journal of Healing and Caring, 9*(1).

Church, D., Hawk, C., Brooks, A., Toukolehto, O., Wren, M., Dinter, I., & Stein, P. (2013). Psychological trauma symptom improvement in veterans using EFT (Emotional Freedom Techniques): A randomized controlled trial. *Journal of Nervous and Mental Disease, 201,* 153–160.

Church, D., & Palmer-Hoffman, J. (2014). TBI symptoms improve after PTSD remediation with Emotional Freedom Techniques. *Traumatology, 20*(3), 172–181.

Church, D., Yount, G., & Brooks, A. J. (2012). The effect of Emotional Freedom Techniques (EFT) on stress biochemistry: A randomized controlled trial. *Journal of Nervous and Mental Disease, 200,* 891–896. doi:10.1097/NMD.0b013e31826b9fc1

Church, D., Yount, G., Rachlin, K., Fox, L., & Nelms, J. (2015). Epigenetic effects of PTSD remediation in veterans using

Clinical EFT (Emotional Freedom Techniques): A randomized controlled trial. Paper presented at the Association for Comprehensive Energy Psychology (ACEP) conference, Reston, VA, May 30, 2015. Submitted for publication.

Craig, G., & Fowlie, A. (1995). *Emotional freedom techniques: The manual.* Sea Ranch, CA: Gary Craig.

Deacon, B. J., & Lickel, J. J. (2009). On the brain disease model of mental disorders. *Behavior Therapist, 32*(6), 113–118.

Diepold, J. H. (2000). Touch and Breathe: An alternative treatment approach with meridian based psychotherapies. *Traumatology, 6*(2), 109–118.

Diepold, J. H., & Goldstein, D. (2008). Thought Field Therapy and qEEG changes in the treatment of trauma: A case study. *Traumatology, 15*(1), 85–93. http://dx.doi.org/10.1177/1534765608325304

Ecker, B., Ticic, R., & Hulley, L. (2012). *Unlocking the emotional brain: Eliminating symptoms at their roots using memory reconsolidation.* New York, NY: Routledge.

Fang, J., Jin, Z., Wang, Y., Li, K., Kong, J., Nixon, E. E., . . . Hui, K. K.-S. (2009). The salient characteristics of the central effects of acupuncture needling: Limbic-paralimbic-neocortical network modulation. *Human Brain Mapping, 30,* 1196–1206. doi:10.1002/hbm.20583

Feinstein, D. (2010). Rapid treatment of PTSD: Why psychological exposure with acupoint tapping may be effective. *Psychotherapy: Theory, Research, Practice, Training, 47,* 385–402. doi:10.1037/a0021171

Feinstein, D. (2012). Acupoint stimulation in treating psychological disorders: Evidence of efficacy. *Review of General Psychology, 16,* 364–380. doi:10.1037/a0028602

Feldenkrais, M. (1984). The master moves. Cupertino, CA: Meta Publications.

Felmingham, K., Williams, L. M., Whitford, T. J., Falconer, E., Kemp, A. H., Peduto, A., & Bryant, R. A. (2009). Duration of posttraumatic stress disorder predicts hippocampal grey matter loss. *Neuroreport, 20*(16), 1402–1406.

Ford, D. E., & Erlinger, T. P. (2004). Depression and C-reactive protein in US adults: data from the Third National Health and Nutrition Examination Survey. *Archives of Internal Medicine, 164*(9), 1010¬–1014.

Freedman, A. M., Kaplan, H. I., & Sadock, B. J. (1975). *Comprehensive textbook of psychiatry.* New York, NY: Williams & Wilkins.

Geronilla, L., McWilliams, M., & Clond, M. (2014, April 17). EFT (Emotional Freedom Techniques) remediates PTSD and psychological symptoms in veterans: A randomized controlled replication trial. Presented at the Grand Rounds, Fort Hood, Killeen, Texas.

Gorey, K. M., & Leslie, D. R. (1997). The prevalence of child sexual abuse: Integrative review adjustment for potential response and measurement biases. *Child Abuse and Neglect, 21*(4), 391–398.

Gurret, J-M., Caufour, C., Palmer-Hoffman, J., & Church, D. (2012). Post-earthquake rehabilitation of clinical PTSD in Haitian seminarians. *Energy Psychology: Theory, Research, and Treatment, 4*(2), 26–34.

Hartung, J., & Stein, P. (2012). Telephone delivery of EFT (Emotional Freedom Techniques) remediates PTSD symptoms in veterans: A randomized controlled trial. *Energy Psychology: Theory, Research, and Treatment, 4*(1), 33–42. doi:10.9769.EPJ.2012.4.1.JH

Hedges, D. W., & Woon, F. L. (2010). Alcohol use and hippocampal volume deficits in adults with posttraumatic stress disorder: A meta-analysis. *Biological Psychology, 84*(2), 163–168.

Hidaka, B. H. (2012). Depression as a disease of modernity: Explanations for increasing prevalence. *Journal of Affective Disorders, 140*(3), 205–214.

Horton, R. (2004). The dawn of McScience. *New York Review of Books, 51*(4), 7–9.

Hui, K. K. S., Liu, J., Marina, O., Napadow, V., Haselgrove, C., Kwong, K. K.,…Makris, N. (2005). The integrated response of the human cerebro-cerebellar and limbic systems to acupuncture stimulation at ST 36 as evidenced by fMRI. *NeuroImage, 27,* 479–496.

Ingelfinger, F. (1977). Health: A matter of statistics of feeling. *New England Journal of Medicine,* February 24, 448–449.

Kanter, E. (2007). Shock and awe hits home. Washington, DC: Physicians for Social Responsibility.

Karatzias, T., Power, K., Brown, K., McGoldrick, T., Begum, M., Young, J.,…Adams, S. (2011). A controlled comparison of the effectiveness and efficiency of two psychological therapies for posttraumatic stress disorder: Eye Movement Desensitization and Reprocessing vs. Emotional Freedom Techniques. *Journal of Nervous and Mental Disease, 199*(6), 372–378.

Kardiner, A. (1941). *The Traumatic Neuroses of War.* New York, NY: P. B. Hoeber.

Katie, Byron. (2002). *Loving what is: Four questions that can change your life.* New York, NY: Harmony Books.

Krystal, J. H., Rosenheck, R. A., Cramer, J. A., Vessicchio, J. C., Jones, K. M., Vertrees, J. E.,…Stock, C. (2011) Adjunctive risperidone treatment for antidepressant-resistant symptoms of chronic military service–related PTSD: A randomized trial. *JAMA, 306*(5), 493–502.

Lambrou, P. T., Pratt, G. J., & Chevalier, G. (2003). Physiological and psychological effects of a mind/body therapy on claustrophobia. *Subtle Energies and Energy Medicine, 14*, 239–251.

McFarlane, A. C., & Van der Kolk, B. (2007). Trauma and its challenge to society. In B. A. van der Kolk, A. C. McFarlane, & L. Weisaeth (Eds.), *Traumatic stress: The effects of overwhelming experience on mind, body, and society* (pp. 24–46). New York, NY: Guilford.

McGowan, P. O., Sasaki, A., Huang, T. C., Unterberger, A., Suderman, M., Ernst C,…Szyf, M. (2008). Promoter-wide hypermethylation of the ribosomal RNA gene promoter in the suicide brain. PLoS One, 3(5), e2085. doi:10.1371/journal.pone.0002085

Monson, C. M., Schnurr, P. P., Resick, P. A., Friedman, M. J., Young-Xu, Y., & Stevens, S. P. (2006). Cognitive processing therapy for veterans with military-related posttraumatic stress disorder. *Journal of Consulting and Clinical Psychology, 74*, 898–907.

Moseley, J. B. (2002). A controlled trial of arthroscopic surgery for osteoarthritis of the knee. *New England Journal of Medicine, 347*, 81.

Nader, K. (2003). Memory traces unbound. *Trends in Neurosciences, 26*(2), 65–72.

Napadow, V., Kettner, N., Liu, J., Li, M., Kwong, K. K., Vangel, M.,…Hui, K. K. (2007). Hypothalamus and amygdala response to acupuncture stimuli in carpal tunnel syndrome. *Pain, 130*(3), 254–266.

Ozer, E. J., Best, S. R., Lipsey, T. L., & Weiss, D. S. (2008). Predictors of posttraumatic stress disorder and symptoms in adults: A meta-analysis. *Psychological Trauma: Theory, Research, Practice, and Policy, 5*(1), 3–36.

Palmer-Hoffman, J., & Brooks, A. J. (2011). Psychological symptom change after group application of Emotional Freedom Techniques (EFT). *Energy Psychology: Theory, Research, and Treatment, 3*(1), 33–38. doi:10.9769. EPJ.2011.3.1.JPH

Peters, J. L., Weisskopf, M. G., Spiro, A., III, Schwartz, J., Sparrow, D., Nie, H.,…Wright, R. J. (2010). Interaction of stress, lead burden, and age on cognition in older men: The VA Normative Aging Study. *Environmental Health Perspectives, 118*(4), 505–510.

Phelps, E. A., & LeDoux, J. E. (2005). Contributions of the amygdala to emotion processing: From animal models to human behavior. *Neuron, 48,* 175–187.

Poulter, M. O, Du, L., Weaver, I. C., Palkovits, M., Faludi, G., Merali, Z., Szyf, M., & Anisman, H. (2008). GABAA receptor promoter hypermethylation in suicide brain: Implications for the involvement of epigenetic processes. *Biological Psychiatry, 64*(8), 645–652. doi:10.1016/j.biopsych.2008.05.028

Rodriguez, T. (2012). Can eye movements treat trauma? Scientific *American, December 19,* 2012. Retrieved from http://www.scientificamerican.com/article/can-eye-movements-treat-trauma

Rogers, C. R. (1957). The necessary and sufficient conditions of therapeutic personality change. *Journal of Consulting Psychology, 21*(2), 95.

Rogers, C. R. (1961). *On becoming a person: A therapist's view of psychotherapy.* New York, NY: Houghton Mifflin.

Rowe, J. E. (2005). The effects of EFT on long-term psychological symptoms. *Counseling and Clinical Psychology, 2,* 104–111.

Scaer, R. C. (2007). *The body bears the burden: Trauma, dissociation, and disease* (2nd ed.). New York, NY: Routledge.

Scaer, R. C. (2012). The dissociation capsule. Retrieved from http://www.traumasoma.com/excerpt1.html

Schlebusch, K. P., Maric-Oehler, W., & Popp, F. A. (2005). Biophotonics in the infrared spectral range reveal acupuncture meridian structure of the body. Journal of Alternative and Complementary Medicine, 11(1), 171–173.

Seal, K. H, Maguen, S., Cohen, B., Gima, K. S., Metzler, T. J., Ren, L.,...Marmar, C. R. (2010). *Journal of Traumatic Stress, 23*(1), 5–16.

Shapiro, F. (1989). Eye movement desensitization and reprocessing: A new treatment for posttraumatic stress disorder. *Journal of Behaviour Therapy and Experimental Psychiatry, 20,* 211–217.

Smith, C. (2012, December 29). Soaring cost of military drugs could hurt budget. *American Statesman.* Retrieved from http://www.statesman.com/news/news/national-govt-politics/the-soaring-cost-of-military-drugs/nThwF

Sroufe, L. A., Egeland, B., Carlson, E. A., & Collins, W. A. (2010). *The development of the person: The Minnesota Study of Risk and Adaptation from Birth to Adulthood.* New York, NY: Guilford.

Stanley, E. A. & Jha, A. P. (2009). Mind fitness and mental armor: Enhancing performance and building warrior resilience. *Joint Force Quarterly, 55,* 144–151.

Stein, P., & Brooks, A. J. (2011). Efficacy of EFT (Emotional Freedom Techniques) provided by coaches vs. licensed therapists in veterans with PTSD. *Energy Psychology: Theory, Research, and Treatment, 3*(1), 11–17.

Sutton, L. K. (2013). Homeward bound—guiding our veterans all the way home: Equipping communities to serve as the front lines of hope & healing. Presented October 19, 2013, at Veterans, Trauma and Treatment conference at Omega Institute, Rhinebeck, NY.

Swingle, P. G., Pulos, L., & Swingle, M. K. (2004). Neurophysiological indicators of EFT treatment of post-traumatic stress. *Subtle Energies and Energy Medicine, 15*(1), 75–86.

Tal, K. (2013, February 26). PTSD: The futile search for the "quick fix." *Scientific American.* Retrieved from http://news.yahoo.com/ptsd-futile-search-quick-fix-163000525.html

Tanielian, T. L., & Jaycox, L. H. (Eds.). (2008). *Invisible wounds of war: Psychological and cognitive injuries, their consequences, and services to assist recovery.* Santa Monica, CA: Rand.

Tedeschi, R. G., & Calhoun, L. G. (2004). Posttraumatic growth: Conceptual foundations and empirical evidence. *Psychological Inquiry, 15*(1), 1–18.

Traquair, H. M. (1944). *An introduction to clinical perimetry* (4th ed.). St. Louis, MO: C. V. Mosby.

Trickett, P. K., Noll, J. G., & Putnam, F. W. (2011). The impact of sexual abuse on female development: Lessons from a multigenerational, longitudinal research study. *Development and Psychopathology, 23*(02), 453¬–476.

Tronick, E., Als, H., Adamson, L., Wise, S., & Brazelton, T. B. (1979). The infant's response to entrapment between contradictory messages in face-to-face interaction. *Journal of the American Academy of Child Psychiatry, 17*(1), 1–13.

Tronick, E. Z. (1989). Emotions and emotional communication in infants. *American Psychologist, 44*(2), 112.

Tym, R., Beaumont, P., & Lioulios, T. (2009). Two persisting pathophysiological visual phenomena following psycho-logical trauma and their elimination with rapid eye movements: A possible refinement of construct PTSD and its visual state marker. *Traumatology, 15*(3), 23–33.

Tym, R., Dyck, M. J., & McGrath, G. (2000). Does a visual perceptual disturbance characterize trauma-related anxiety syndromes? *Journal of Anxiety Disorders, 14*(4), 377–394.

U.S. Department of Health and Human Services. (2012). *Child maltreatment 2011*. Washington, DC: Administration for Children and Families, Administration on Children, Youth and Families, Children's Bureau. Retrieved from http://www.acf.hhs.gov

Van der Kolk, B. A. (2014). *The body keeps the score: Brain, mind, and body in the healing of trauma*. New York, NY: Viking.

Vasterling, J. J., & Brewin, C. R. (Eds.). (2005). *Neuropsychology of PTSD: Biological, cognitive, and clinical perspectives*. New York, NY: Guilford.

Vickers, A. J., Cronin, A. M., Maschino, A. C., Lewith, G., MacPherson, H., Foster, N. E.,…Linde, K. (2012, October 22). Acupuncture for chronic pain: Individual patient data meta-analysis. *Archives of Internal Medicine, 172*(19), 1444–1453. doi:10.1001/archinternmed.2012.3654

Wells, S., Polglase, K., Andrews, H. B., Carrington, P., & Baker, A. H. (2003). Evaluation of a meridian-based intervention, Emotional Freedom Techniques (EFT), for reducing specific phobias of small animals. *Journal of Clinical Psychology, 59*, 943–966. doi:10.1002/jclp.10189

Whitaker, R. (2011). *Anatomy of an epidemic: Magic bullets, psychiatric drugs, and the astonishing rise of mental illness in America*. New York, NY: Random House.

Wolpe, J. (1958). *Psychotherapy by reciprocal inhibition*. Palo Alto, CA: Stanford University Press.

Index

A

abreaction, 289
acceptance phrase, 142–144
    soft language and,
      145–148
Adams, Ann, 153, 160
affirmation, EFT, 92–95
Amias, Angela, 22
anger, EFT and, 118, 147, 209,
    230–231, 246, 251
ankle points, 137
apex effect, 150–151
aspects, EFT and, 105–107

B

baby finger point, 129
Basic Recipe, EFT, 81
    example applied to general
      description, 156–158
    example applied to specific
      memory, 159–160
below the nipple point, 128
betrayal, 249, 251

blood pressure changes, 217
body language changes, 216
Borrowing Benefits, 151–154
breathing changes, 216
Brenda, EFT client, 160–164

C

Callahan, Dr. Roger, 26, 150
Carrington, Dr. Patricia, 149
chasing the pain, 58, 171,
    197–199
chin point, 98–99
Clark, Tana, 133–134
cognitive shift, 75, 77,
    178–180, 191, 218
collarbone point, 98–99
core issue, 107–108
cravings, EFT for, 93
crying, 192, 217

D

Dinter, Ingrid, 256

dissociation, 42, 56–56, 92,
    183–189
do-it-yourself EFT, 389–304

E
EFT (Emotional Freedom
    Techniques)
    affirmation, 92–95
    anger and, 118, 143,
        147, 209, 230–231,
        246, 251
    Basic Recipe, 81
    combat PTSD, for
        239–262
    complications, 211
    creation of, 26
    do-it-yourself, 263–278
    EFT points, 97–99
    EFT points, optional,
        127–131
    generalization effect and,
        105, 108–111, 117,
        183
    guilt and, 75, 106–107,
        118, 142
    incorrect tapping, 151, 210
    preemptive, 246
    Psychological Reversal
        and, 90–92
    Reminder Phrase, 99–100
    self-talk and, 212
    Sequence, 98–99
    Setup, 89–90
    signs that it's working,
        120–122
    tail-enders, 213–215
    writings on your
        walls, 212

The EFT Manual, 26, 32,
    81, 272
eyebrow point, 98–99

F
facial muscles relax, 217
Farrell, Pat, 268
Feinstein, David, 77
flashbacks, 23, 96, 156, 159,
    160–164, 167, 222, 234,
    275
freeze response, 43

G
Gamut point, 70, 132
Gamut Procedure, 131–133
generalization effect, 105,
    108–111, 117, 183
guilt, EFT and, 75, 106–107,
    118, 142

H
Hessel, Evan, veteran, 239
Hurricane Katrina, 229
hypervigilance, 56, 147

I
index finger point, 129
intensity, measuring, 86–88
intensity meter, 87

K
Karate Chop point, 28, 97
Kenny, Lindsay, 247–248

L
Look, Dr. Carol, 153, 263
Lorenz, Lori, 233–234

Louie-Handelman,
    Constance, 245
Lyon, Angela Treat, 149

M
Marina, Rebecca, 228–229
measuring intensity, 86–88
Miner, Edward, 164
Mountrose, Dr. Jane, 149
Mountrose, Dr. Phillip, 149
Movie Technique, 111–116

N–O
9 Gamut Procedure, 131–133
Olli, veteran, 242
optional EFT points, 127–131

P
pain gets worse, 219
pain moves, 219
Patefield, Bob, 275
Paulette, EFT client, 229–231
PCL-M (PTSD Checklist–
    Military), 184, 240–241
Personal Peace Procedure,
    117–120
points, tapping, 97–99
polarity reversal, 90–92
posture changes, 216–217
preemptive EFT tapping,
    246
Psychological Reversal,
    90–92
PTSD
    conventional therapy
        for, 66
    EFT treatment, evidence
        for, 33–35

PTSD Checklist–Military
    (PCL-M), 184
pulse changes, 217–218

R
rape trauma, 22–25
Reminder Phrase, EFT, 99–101
Reversal, Psychological,
    90–92
Rogers, Carl, 94, 194
Rogers, Lisa, 271

S
Scott, Winston "Brad," 18
self-talk, 212–213
Sequence, EFT, 98–99
Setup, EFT, 89–90
side of eye point, 98–99
sigh, 216
sinus draining, 217
Sore Spot, 135–136
Story Technique, 111–116

T
TAB (Touch and Breathe)
    method, 201–202
tail-enders, 213–215
TBI (traumatic brain
    injury), 34
Tearless Trauma Technique,
    186–188
Tell the Story Technique,
    111–116
temperature changes, 218
temporomandibular joint
    problems (TMJ), 251
terrorist attacks, EFT and,
    221–228

thumb point, 128
tinnitus, 251, 253
TMJ (temporomandibular joint problems), 251
top of head point, 136–137
Touch and Breathe (TAB) method, 201–202
trauma, criteria/characteristics, 38, 172
traumatic brain injury, 34

U
under the arm point, 98–99
under eye point, 98–99
U.S. Department of Veterans Affairs, 273

V
V.A. (Veterans Affairs/ Administration), 247
veterans, combat, EFT for, 239–262
vibrating energy, 218
voice changes, 216

W
Watch the Movie Technique, 111–116
Wilkes, Rick, 207
World Trade Center, 187, 221–228
wrist points, 137
writings on your walls, 212

Y
yawn, 216